CHOOSING YOUR WAY THROUGH THE WORLD'S ANCIENT PAST

Anne E. Schraff

illustrated by Steven Meyers

J. Weston Walch, Publisher
Portland, Maine

Users' Guide
to
Walch Reproducible Books

As part of our general effort to provide educational materials which are as practical and economical as possible, we have designated this publication a "reproducible book." The designation means that purchase of the book includes purchase of the right to limited reproduction of all pages on which this symbol appears:

Here is the basic Walch policy: We grant to individual purchasers of this book the right to make sufficient copies of reproducible pages for use by all students of a single teacher. This permission is limited to a single teacher, and does not apply to entire schools or school systems, so institutions purchasing the book should pass the permission on to a single teacher. Copying of the book or its parts for resale is prohibited.

Any questions regarding this policy or requests to purchase further reproduction rights should be addressed to:

Permissions Editor
J. Weston Walch, Publisher
P.O. Box 658
Portland, ME 04104-0658

—J. Weston Walch, Publisher

1 2 3 4 5 6 7 8 9 10

ISBN 0-8251-1907-3

Printed in the United States of America

Contents

The Adventures

To the Teacher

Choosing Your Way Through the World's Ancient Past is a series of twenty adventure stories. Beginning with the dim past, when cave-dwelling peoples began to migrate and separate into the major racial groups, and concluding with the decline of Roman civilization, these adventures give students a first-hand experience of ancient history. By the process of choice, the student has the chance to feel the fears of the cave dweller battling wild animals and daring to take the first courageous steps toward civilization. The student is invited to tame a wolf, leap over a wild bull in Crete, learn from Socrates, and share in Rome's glory and decline.

Though Western civilization is highlighted, Eastern adventures—in the Indus Valley city of Mohenjo-Daro, among Persian princes, and in the Han dynasty of China—are included as well. Although the stories are fictional, all of the historical details are accurate. The fear of the Spartan youth, the triumph of the Greek athlete, and the horrors of the Carthaginian siege bring an exciting "you are there" quality to the study of ancient history.

This book is intended to introduce periods of ancient history to students in a way which will make it more relevant to them. It is often hard for students to understand how peoples of so long ago shared common human emotions and dreams with present-day people. Since we can only guess at many details of prehistoric life, students should be told that the early stories are based on theories about what probably happened. It must also be emphasized that many changes, such as the introduction of agriculture, came very slowly.

By becoming an ancient person, the student will make choices and experience consequences which bring triumph, tragedy, or just a different kind of future. The wrong choice might lead a student into a Roman Senate chamber and assassination, or to the sands of Africa to be devoured by the wild animals destined for the Roman arena.

As a supplement to their classroom textbook, these adventures will spark the imagination of students and bring to life such distant peoples as the Babylonians, Sumerians, and Egyptians. All the different traditions are treated with respect; commonly accepted virtues of bravery, honesty, compassion, and individual excellence are emphasized. Within these pages move such famous figures as Socrates, Alexander the Great, and Hammurabi, but the main character in these adventures is the average person.

Each adventure is supplemented by a short reading about interesting, important, or unusual sidelights of the era. This material is entirely factual. There are matching or true/false questions for each adventure. There are also suggestions for group and individual activities for each story.

Other recommended activities for all the stories include the following:

- Students might keep a written record of the pages they chose and what happened to them in their adventures.
- The teacher might conduct regular discussions among groups who chose different courses of action and ask questions like, "What usually guided your decision?"
- Students might be asked at the conclusion of several stories what they have learned about decision-making and their own attitudes so far. At the end of the book, the question could be asked again.
- Vocabulary may be reviewed before each story is read.
- At the end of the book, the class might discuss which of the civilizations seemed most, and least, like our own. Which ones had the most to teach us?
- The characters in these adventures are not gender-specific. The teacher might pose this question: Could all the characters be either male or female? Students should be urged to identify with the character even if the person seems to be of the opposite sex. For example, girls should feel free to pretend to be warriors, even though in ancient times warriors were generally male.
- At the end of the book students might write an essay on their favorite ancient civilization. What values do they admire from that civilization? Are these values still evident in our society?

Answer Key

1. In the Beginning

1. d
2. e
3. b
4. a
5. c

2. The First Farmers

1. T
2. T
3. F
4. T
5. T

3. A Person's Best Friend

1. T
2. T
3. F
4. F
5. T

4. The Surprising Sumerians

1. c
2. e
3. a
4. d
5. b

5. Babylon and Beyond

1. c
2. d
3. a
4. e
5. b

6. Indus Valley Decision

1. d
2. c
3. a
4. e
5. b

7. Careers in Crete

1. c
2. a
3. c
4. d
5. b

8. The Great Pharaoh and the Slaves

1. c
2. a
3. d
4. e
5. b

9. A Gift in the Land of Canaan

1. d
2. b
3. a
4. e
5. c

10. An Athenian Dream

1. e
2. c
3. a
4. d
5. b

11. A Spartan Life

1. c
2. e
3. a
4. d
5. b

12. The Persian Plot

1. c
2. a
3. b
4. d
5. e

13. The Great Teacher

1. b
2. a
3. e
4. d
5. c

14. Riding with Alexander the Great

1. c
2. d
3. a
4. b
5. e

15. The People of Han

1. T
2. T
3. F
4. T
5. F

16. The Last Days of Carthage

1. b
2. e
3. d
4. a
5. c

17. Cleopatra, Queen of the Nile

1. e
2. b
3. a
4. d
5. c

18. The Persecution

1. d
2. a
3. c
4. e
5. b

19. The Fall of Rome

1. F
2. T
3. T
4. T
5. F

20. The Empire Moves East

1. e
2. c
3. a
4. d
5. b

In the Beginning— 60,000 Years Ago

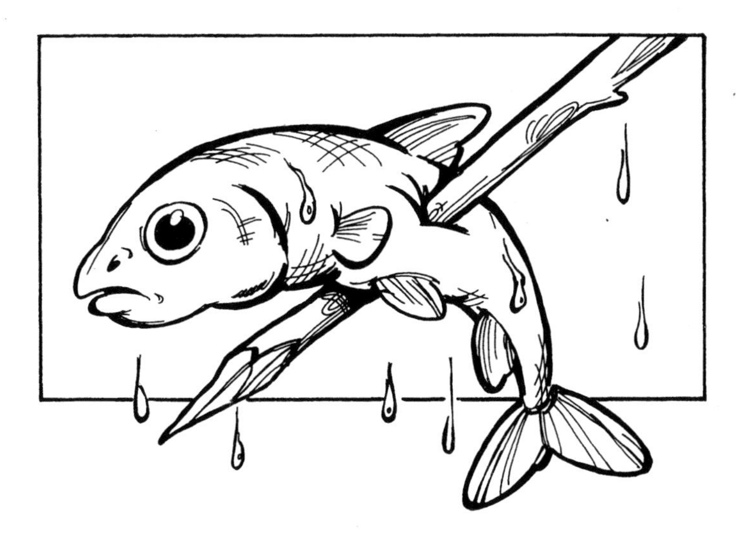

You live on the hot, sandy shores of an African river. Your home is an oval hut made from branches pushed into the sand and propped up with rocks. The hut is covered with brush. It protects you from the hot sun and heavy rains.

Stooping near your hut, you skin a rabbit for dinner. You use a pebble tool, a natural stone chipped to have sharp edges. You don't have many tools, just a scraper and a v-shaped rock used as a cleaver.

Sometimes you fish, using a pointed stick to spear them. But you like the meat of rabbits and shrews better than fish. You also like juicy wild berries and roots.

You take the skinned rabbit into your hut. You have a small hearth in your hut. It is only a circle of stones to build a fire on. Now you drive a stick through the rabbit and turn it over the flames.

You keep your fire going all the time. You need flaming sticks to drive wild animals away from your hut. And roasting meat makes it tastier and more tender. You sometimes lose your fire. A wind can blow it out. Then you must work long and hard to make a new one. Sometimes twirling a sharp stick in the hollow of a flat stick makes a spark.

Sometimes you eat raw meat. You must chew and chew until your jaws ache. But today a good smell fills your hut. How wonderful the roasted meat smells! When you are no longer hungry and there is very little meat left, you go outside. You kneel by a spring and scoop up a drink of water.

You have lived here all your life. The river is like a member of your family. But now you are a strong young adult. You wonder if there is a better place to live than here. In recent years the game animals have become less common. Where have they gone to? You worry that there will not be enough to eat next year. You must travel and find where the animals have gone.

When you climb into a tall thorn tree for a better view, you see greener land to the south. To the north, the land rises. Perhaps the herds have gone there. What about the land to the east? Should you explore there?

- *If you go south, turn to page 3.*
- *If you go north, turn to page 4.*
- *If you go east, turn to page 6.*

Find out what your fate is!

You begin your journey south along the river. You are nervous as you walk. You have never been this far from your hut before. Just ahead, in a clump of thick trees, you see a large yellow piece of fruit hanging from a branch. You pull the fruit down and taste it. It is sweet and juicy. It is so much larger than the small berries you are used to. It is like a breadfruit—sweet and starchy.

You stoop and peer into the river. There are more fish in this part of the river. It is easy to spear one. In nearby trees monkeys scream and chatter. This part of the river is very rich in animal and plant life.

You return to your old hut and gather a few tools. Your spouse and your son and daughter place live coals from the fire in a pot which they carry with them, so that you always have fire. You will all go south along the river to find a better place to live.

After many days of travel you find a place for your new hut. You drive branches into the soft earth and soon have a brush-covered hut. You start your hearth fire and get used to your new home.

Your children enjoy watching bright green parrots screeching in the trees. But there is little time to watch parrots. Everyone must work hard. A new hand-axe must be made. There are animals to be skinned and fruit to gather.

You find that life is better here. Food is more plentiful and the weather is warmer.

But perhaps if you went even farther south, life would be better still.

Every few years you travel farther south. Your children grow tall and strong. There are joys and sorrows. One of your small sons drowns in the river. One of your daughters is killed by a prowling wildcat.

By the time you build your last hut, you have moved to a very hot southern woodland. The sun burns down. You have turned darker. Your children and grandchildren are darker, too.

You had thick, dark hair as a young adult, but your descendants will have thicker and woolier hair. This will protect their heads from the strong rays of the sun. You turned darker from years of strong sunlight, but your descendants will be much darker than you ever were. Nature will allow the darkest children to be the healthiest, and even darker children will be born of them. Dark skin provides more protection from the hot sun.

Your descendants will be the parents of many African peoples.

■ ***Turn to page 9.***

You follow a herd north with your spouse and children. You carry a few tools and your pot of coals for fire. You stop for a few months or a few years in many places.

One day you reach a great sea[1] which lies beside a large sandy area.[2] This is a good place and you live here for a long time. You draw many fish from the sea. Where the sea is narrow you can see the far shore. What is life like in that place? You decide to swim across the water. You and your spouse and children scramble ashore and look around at this different land.[3] You will stay here. You build a hut edged with rings of boulders and make a new fire.

You are surprised how much colder this land is. You cover your floors with skins, and you wrap yourself in skins, too. It is not like the hot land you left long ago. You are eager to keep your fire going all the time in winter.

Your food is different, too. You hunt deer and wild pigs. Sometimes you can find nothing but rabbits or rats, but there is always food.

"The meat of the deer is good," says your spouse as you sit by the fire in your hut.

"This place is good," you agree. You look at your two children. The youngest one is weak. The cold wind is not good for him. "That boy is not well," you say.

"He will get used to this new land," says your spouse. You nod. But you worry when the next winter comes. The winds are fierce. One morning your son does not wake up. You and your spouse go out to dig a grave. You line it with sweet-smelling grasses and some flowers that grow here even in winter. You put your son's hand-axe in the grave with him. You believe he can use this when he wakes up in the next life. You believe there is life after death.

You and your spouse have two more children, both girls. They are very strong. When your children grow up and marry others who have come north, many grandchildren are born. Your grandchildren move still farther north and east.[4]

(continued on page 5)

[1] Mediterranean

[2] Sahara Desert

[3] Spain

[4] France, Germany, and elsewhere in Europe

When you began to travel north from your African river, you were dark-skinned and dark-haired. Your dark hair was curly. But your descendants will look different from you. The sun is not so hot here, so lighter-skinned people will live longer and have more children. Your descendants will have lighter and lighter skin. The curly black hair that protected you from the hot sun will die out. Your descendants will have straighter and lighter hair.

Your descendants will be the parents of many European peoples.

■ ***Turn to page 9.***

You and your spouse and children carry your pot of coals for fire and tools east. The land is drier here than in your home. You come to a vast land with few plants. You grow very fearful. You cannot find food! You must trap lizards to keep from starving.

One day you see a large animal in the brush. It is a rhinoceros. You drive him into a wall of rocks with fiery sticks and kill him with your spear. Now you will have food for many days. You rest and eat until you can eat no more. Then you move on, following another herd of animals. Always you are going farther east.

You work for several days to make new tools. Your old tools are too dull and old to be of use anymore. You make a fine new hand-axe, chipping flakes from a stone to shape it. Finally you have a good, sharp tool. Now you can skin and cut up animals more quickly.

You stay only a few days in some places. You eat plenty of deer and wild pigs. But sometimes there is nothing to eat but the insects that live beneath rocks.

For the first time in your life you see snow. At first you are terror-stricken. Why does the rain come down in white, icy pieces? "Cold! So cold!" you gasp.

Luckily you soon kill a bear. You and your spouse and children huddle in your hut under the bearskin. Even with your fire going, you are numb with the cold. You are afraid you will die here.[5]

"We must go home," your spouse moans. "Too cold!"

You look outside the hut. Icy snow is blowing. It is too cold to travel. But if you stay here you are afraid you will turn to ice. Maybe it will get colder and colder and even the fire will freeze. Maybe you will all turn as hard as stone.

"We must go," cries your spouse. The children are crying with the cold, too.

■ ***If you go, turn to page 7.***

■ ***If you stay, turn to page 8.***

[5] Asian highlands

You wrap yourself in bearskin robes and go outside. Your spouse and children follow you. One of your sons is weak. One is strong. You must carry the weak one.

The wind is so strong you quickly grow tired. You must stop and rest.

"We will die if we stop," your spouse says.

Soon you are lucky enough to find a small cave. But you cannot make a fire. It is so cold and you are sleepy. Maybe if you all huddle together and go to sleep it will be warmer in the morning. Then you can try to find your way to a warmer place.

In the morning you and your spouse are dead. Your youngest son is dead, too. Only your strong son still lives.

The frightened boy runs from the cave. He runs back to your hut. The fire still burns there. He huddles by the flames and gets warm. He eats some meat and cries with fear and grief.

In a few days the snow is gone. The boy hunts and kills a large rabbit. He eats again and grows stronger. The weather is warmer and the earth grows softer. The boy goes to the cave and carries the bodies of his parents and his brother to a meadow. He spends many hours digging graves.

He buries you and your spouse and your son in grass-filled graves. He spreads the finest boughs he can find over your graves.

Somehow the boy survives alone until one afternoon when he meets a man and woman in search of antelope. He joins up with them and they all move south.

The boy does not remember the way home, but he travels to a warmer place.[6] He settles there. As he grows up, he remembers the lessons you and your spouse taught him. He tells his children of his brave parents who traveled to a new land.

■ ***Turn to page 9.***

[6] North Africa

"No!" you cry out. "It is too cold to leave the fire."

You huddle around the fire for three days. The last of the deer meat is eaten.

You peer from your hut to see a clear blue sky. It is still cold, but it is warmer. The snow is blowing away at last.

"Good!" you shout.

You and your spouse work very hard now. You hunt two large pigs. You skin them and roast the meat. The delicious, juicy meat brings strength to all of you. Even your weak son is stronger now. You gather branches to burn in your hearth and the hut crackles with warmth. You are very glad you stayed here.

Other hunters come, and you all follow a great herd of mammoth. You are lucky. You bring down a large beast. You will use its meat as food. From the hide you will have clothing. The bones of the mammoth will make fuel for your fire. The fat of the mammoth will burn and light your hut.

Soon you move again, following a herd of deer. Ever eastward you go.

When your sons are grown one moves into central Asia and another reaches China. The daughters who were born to you and your spouse also move to central Asia.

After many years, your descendants will look very different from you. You have dark skin and dark curly hair. But your descendants will develop flatter, broader faces. A fold of skin will develop over their upper eyelids. This will protect their eyes from the sun's glare on the snow. The fold will give their eyes a slanted look. Your descendants will have lighter skin in this colder climate. Their hair will be straighter than your hair was.

Your descendants will populate Asia, and spread over the rest of the world.

■ ***Turn to page 9.***

Different Peoples

Back in the Stone Age, our common ancestors were probably medium dark with long, dark hair. Then, as small groups moved around to different climates, they began to change in appearance. Darker skin did better in Africa, so darker people had more and healthier children. Soon Africans were very dark-skinned. Lighter skin did better in colder climates. Whatever kind of hair and skin we have today is not important, but back then it was a matter of survival.

We are all from the same family of humanity. Our Stone Age relatives must have had a lot of courage, for wherever they went life was hard. Our original human family was once very small, probably living in Africa. Now we are many, living all over the world.

Matching

______ 1. This helped against sun glare on snow — a) cleavers

______ 2. This helped in a hot climate — b) light skin

______ 3. This helped in a cold climate — c) tender

______ 4. V-shaped rocks were used as — d) extra fold of skin over eyes

______ 5. Roasting meat made it tastier and more — e) dark skin

Group Activities

1. Collect natural rocks, some of which are whole and some broken. Bring them to school, arrange them on a table, and discuss how you could have used these rocks in the Stone Age.
2. Look at a large map of the world. Starting from Kenya, where some believe the earliest people lived, draw three bright paths with felt pens. One should lead toward Asia, one toward Europe, and one into southern Africa.
3. Discuss Stone Age life. Which parts of it were most difficult? Which parts might have been easier than our present-day lives?

Individual Activities

1. We learn about Stone Age people by uncovering places where people lived. These places are called digs. Make a clay-filled box and press in items such as a fork, pencil, or screwdriver. Notice how the shapes that are left tell you a lot, even when the object is removed.
2. Write a paragraph about Stone Age tools.
3. If a Stone Age person came into your classroom, what three questions would you ask him or her? Write them down.

The First Farmers—10,000 B.C.

You are a young Southeast Asian. As long as you can remember you have hunted and gathered to live. You have always worried whether there would be enough food. Would the animals be as plentiful as in past seasons? Would the seeds and roots wither, or be eaten by wild animals, leaving you with nothing?

Now your brother calls to you. "Look," he says in an excited voice. "See how the grain grows thickly in this spot! There is enough here to feed my family for many weeks."

"That is where we throw the scraps from our meals," you say.

"Ah. The dirt here is good. If I put in more grains I could have food when I wanted. I would not have to wander about looking for wild plants to eat," your brother says.

How wonderful this would be! No more tiresome food-gathering. No more sharing your grain with whatever bird or animal or stranger picks and eats it first. If you raised grain near your house, you could watch it and chase away birds.

But what of all the time you spend hunting? Could you raise your meat as well? You often hunt the wild jungle fowl. The meat of the fowl is tasty. How good it would be to have meat at your door.

You have often heard the wild jungle fowl crowing at dawn. Sometimes when you carry wild grain home, you drop some near your house. You have seen the fowl gathering it. The more you drop, the more jungle fowl come. And they come again the next day. They seem to remember where food is available.

If you draw them closer and closer to your house, they will stay. They will no longer be wild jungle fowl. They will be your chickens. You can snatch one for your meal whenever you need it.

Perhaps your brother should cultivate the wild grain and you should try to draw in a flock of jungle fowl. Or would it be more sensible to raise grain?

■ ***If you raise grain, turn to page 13.***

■ ***If you tame the jungle fowl, turn to page 14.***

Find out what your fate is!

You decide to raise grain. You rake at the earth with a pointed stick near your scrap pile. You drop in seeds carefully.

"What foolishness," says your spouse. "The wild grain must grow as it will. You cannot command it to grow where it is handy. Nothing will grow in that spot. Your back will ache."

"We shall see," you say.

"It is like asking the sky to send rain on command," your spouse says. "It like trying to order the river to flow as you want it to go, or choosing the song a bird will sing."

"We shall see," you say.

After a rain you see green shoots in your new garden. You get down on your knees to look more closely. Could your grain be growing? Yes, you are sure of it! You get up and run to your house, shouting and waving your arms. "The grain grows! I have made the grain grow where we want it!"

Your spouse is roasting a wild pig. "I will see for myself," says your spouse, not really believing you.

By the time both of you reach the garden, a very large rabbit is eating there. You run toward it, shouting, "Away! Go away!"

Your spouse looks for the green shoots. "There is nothing growing here," your spouse says with a sharp laugh.

"But there was. The rabbit ate the young shoots."

"Your time would be better spent hunting the rabbit. We need meat when the wild pig is gone. We can always find wild grain when we need it," says your spouse. "Wild grain grows where it will. We are not magicians. We cannot command the forces of nature."

You feel very sad. You feel angry, too. Should you plant again and this time watch out for wild animals? Or should you give up and go hunting while there is still light in the sky?

■ ***If you plant again, turn to page 15.***

■ ***If you go hunting, turn to page 18.***

Every day you toss the wild seed a bit closer to your house. The jungle fowl seem more plentiful every day. When you go near them at first, they scatter wildly. You try the next day and they scatter just a few yards away. Then, finally, you can almost walk among them. They ignore you and pick at the seeds.

"Look," you say to your brother. "Many jungle fowl gather here. I do not frighten them anymore. It shall be easy to snatch one when my family is hungry."

Your brother nods, but then he says, "If the jungle fowl gather in such large numbers, will the wild beasts who hunt them gather, too? What if the tiger comes to your door and eats us as well as the jungle fowl?"

You laugh. "The tiger has other things to eat. He can eat the monkeys. What does the tiger want with a small chicken?" you say.

"But the monkeys can climb trees and mock the tiger," your brother points out. "Then the tiger is very hungry and he looks here."

"The chickens can fly from the tiger," you say.

"Yes, and then the hungry tiger will eat my son or your daughter," says your brother. "I fear living where wild fowl gather."

"You worry for nothing," you say. "It will be so good to have meat whenever we want it. The jungle fowl will increase. When I can find no wild pig, I can kill chickens and my family will eat their fill."

Each day your flock grows. You are so pleased. The jungle fowl is a tasty bird and there is always enough white and dark meat for your family.

Then, one day, your brother's fears come true. You hear a great uproar from your jungle fowl and they are flying all about, into the branches of the trees. You come rushing out and a tiger jumps at you, red jaws open! You swing at the beast with your hand-axe. It is a young tiger and he is easily frightened. A clever old cat would be harder to scare. But a pile of bloody feathers tells you this tiger has already tasted your jungle fowl. He will come back for more once he has tasted here. Or perhaps he will just go away and be content to sneak up on monkeys. Should you try to hunt him down and kill him?

■ ***If you hunt the tiger, turn to page 16.***

■ ***If not, turn to page 17.***

You plant more grain, but this time you must not let the rabbit steal from you. And what of the other pests? They will gather in your garden and eat everything you have.

"I must watch my garden by day and sleep beside the plants at night," you say.

"How foolish," says your spouse. "At night you will be cold. You will get sick with a fever and die."

"I will wrap myself in animal skins," you say.

That night you go outside and sleep in your garden. You miss the warmth of your hut. Nothing comes to eat your green shoots all night, but in the early dawn you see rabbits! You leap up with a stick and chase them away.

You have learned something. The rabbits come to eat in the very early morning and then late in the afternoon. When the sun is setting and just after it rises is the most likely time of danger for your tender green shoots.

You plan to be very alert at those times. Soon you know when to sleep in your hut and when to be in the garden with a stick.

Your spouse is surprised to see how the garden is growing. "We will not go hungry this season. We shall have enough wild grain for all our meals," says your spouse.

Your neighbors come and admire your garden. Pretty soon they decide to do the same thing as you have done, and changes come to your life.

You used to spend long hours searching for wild grain. When the grain was scarce you would leave your hut and go somewhere else and build another hut. Now you will not have to leave here. Others decide to stay, too, and where a few huts once stood, there is now a small village.

You grind the grain to make flour. There is time to talk with neighbors while you work. Searching the fields for wild grain was very lonely. You enjoy having others around. Life becomes more interesting.

You plant other crops. You raise beans and peas and cucumbers and other grains. You have much better food to eat. All this is new and wonderful. You don't have to eat the same thing every day. One day you may have a cucumber, crisp and juicy. The next day you might eat beans. You can store your food and even trade it with others for chickens or pigs.

You have become one of the world's first farmers.

■ ***Turn to page 19.***

You set out through the forest after the tiger. You carry your spear tightly in your hand. Your knuckles are white because you hold the spear so tightly. You have brought down animals as large as the rhinoceros with your spear. But the rhinoceros does not move as swiftly as the tiger; the tiger could turn around and eat you!

The monkeys screech from the trees as you go by. Or does something else make them cry?

There is the tiger, as bright as a fire before you!

You hurl your spear mightily. Oh no! You miss! It falls short of its mark. The angry, snarling tiger comes toward you. You see the sharp white teeth and the red throat!

You clamber up a tree. You are struggling to save your life now. If the tiger gets you, you are doomed, for you have dropped your spear.

The tiger would climb the tree after you, but you have chosen a spindly tree. Now the tiger waits at the bottom.

Your family probably thinks you have been killed and eaten. Maybe they will have to grieve for you after all.

Finally the tiger goes away and you can safely come down. You snatch up your fallen spear and head toward home. As you run, you meet two other hunters.

"Tiger! Tiger!" they shout, pointing to a nearby cave.

You join them and run to the cave. One of the hunters has a burning torch. You corner the tiger in the cave with the torch. The tiger charges and your arm is slashed. But the other hunters kill him with their spears.

You go home to your hut with a bleeding arm. Your spouse looks at the wound and then gathers herbs and some mud from the river. The herbs and mud will make a pack for your wound.

Your arm begins to heal in a few days. You feel very good that the tiger is dead. You are given one-third of the tiger skin after it is skinned. It will be very soft for your new baby daughter to lie on.

"Now the tiger will not eat our chickens," you say to your spouse and your brother.

"There are other tigers," says your brother.

"My arm is healing. I will protect my chickens and my family with my spear," you say.

You have become one of the world's first animal raisers. From now on, people will raise the animals they need more and more. The need to hunt will grow less and less.

■ ***Turn to page 19.***

You decide not to follow the tiger. It is very dangerous to stalk a tiger. And maybe he will never come back here. He is a young tiger. Maybe he will not be clever enough to remember where the jungle fowl are.

Two nights pass and you are feeling very safe. But on the third night you hear your chickens squawking. You grab your spear and rush outside. Bloody chicken feathers are flying as the tiger moves among your birds. With a scream of rage you lunge at the tiger. He leaps to safety and vanishes into the woodland. Your heart is pounding in fury. You are filled with hatred for the dumb beast. You do not stop to think that he is only following his wild nature.

At the edge of the woodland you look around for the tiger. But he is behind you! He jumps onto your back and his jaws rip your shoulder. You scream loudly. Other hunters come from nearby huts. But when they find you the tiger has gone and you are badly mauled.

The hunters carry you the short distance back to your hut. Your spouse comes out and helps take you inside. You are bleeding very heavily from your terrible wound.

Your spouse gathers medicinal herbs and makes a pack to stop the bleeding. But the next day you are very feverish. You are afraid that you will die. You moan and toss on your animal-skin bed.

In the morning you do not wake up. Your spouse and children dig a grave for you. They bury you with sweet-smelling herbs and flowers. You are the third person this year who has been killed by wild animals. It is a very common way to die here. Very few people grow old.

Your spouse and oldest daughter continue to care for the flock of chickens. They watch them closely and scare away the wild animals with burning torches. Grain is grown here, too, and soon the few huts become a village. These people become some of the world's first farmers. But it all comes too late for you to enjoy.

■ ***Turn to page 19.***

Your spouse is right. Hunting and gathering is easier than trying to raise crops. You walk for a short distance before you see a wild pig running through the woodland. You run, too. The taste of roast pig is very good indeed. It is your favorite meat. The flesh is so juicy. You can already taste it!

You hear the shouts of other hunters. Is someone else after this same wild pig? You saw the beast first!

You see the pig now. It is cornered by two hunters.

"It is my kill to take," you shout. "I have been tracking the beast."

The other two hunters glare fiercely at you.

"The kill is to the hunter who makes it. Our families are hungry. We have been without meat for a long time!" says the oldest and fiercest-looking of the two hunters.

The squealing pig is killed. The hunters tie its hooves together and begin loading it on a stout branch to carry it home. But you will not let this happen. It is not fair!

You wave your spear in a menacing way. You hope at least they will share the meat with you. But it is two against one. "Go away or die like the pig!" growls the old hunter.

You will not go away. You run at the hunters with your spear held aloft. The younger hunter picks up a stone and dashes it against your head! Your spear flies from your hand. You fall into a brushy ravine.

When you wake up your head hurts. Your hair is matted with blood. But you are not seriously hurt. The other hunters have gone off with the pig they killed—*your pig*! But there is no sense thinking anymore about that.

You spend half the day looking for meat. You come upon a mole and kill it. What a poor meal the scrawny little creature will make. But it is better than nothing at all.

You are still very hungry after you share the mole meat with your family. You wonder if raising grain and even trying to raise jungle fowl might be a good idea after all.

Maybe tomorrow you will try again. Hunting and gathering is not such a good life either—especially when your head hurts as much as yours does.

■ ***Turn to page 19.***

When People Got Together

Early people roamed around in very small groups looking for plants and animals to eat. Often they saw only their family members for long periods. But when people began to raise crops and animals, it was the beginning of villages and towns and cities. People could now stay in one place and trade and talk and work together. Having people gathered in one place allowed for different skills to emerge. A person who was good at making tools became a toolmaker, for example. People working together made it easier to deal with food shortages and wild animal attacks. Farming gave people the chance to share their burdens, their joys, and their whole lives. Life became more interesting and a lot more satisfying. It was the beginning of civilization.

True/False

_______ 1. Wild grain grew better by rubbish piles.

_______ 2. Farming led to more people living in one place.

_______ 3. Before farming began there was less hunting.

_______ 4. One of the animals raised in Southeast Asia was the jungle fowl, or chicken.

_______ 5. Farming was the beginning of civilization.

Group Activities

1. Using a large map, find the following areas of the world where farming is thought to have begun on a large scale in ancient times:

Mexico	Indus Valley
Peru	Far East
Near East	Southeast Asia

2. Do you think the development of farming gave people more, or less, free time? Discuss what they probably did with their free time.
3. People who lived about 6,000 years ago began making jewelry from pretty stones and shells. They drilled holes in the stones and shells and strung them into necklaces. Make some jewelry from stones, shells, or other natural objects.

Individual Activities

1. Imagine you are being pursued by a tiger. In one paragraph tell what you would do.
2. Prehistoric people of about 30,000 years ago painted the walls of their caves using natural colors, such as green from leaves and red from the earth. Using only natural colors, color or paint a picture.
3. Go to the library and find pictures of the prehistoric paintings in the caves at Altamira, Spain, and Lascaux, France. Describe what the paintings look like to you in one paragraph.

A Person's Best Friend—8500 B.C.

You are a young hunter in northern Europe. You also fish, and when meat is scarce you eat fish gladly. You have a dugout canoe made from a log. You fish with a spear that has barbed prongs. You carved the prongs from the antlers of a deer.

Your family has been hungry all week. You searched the forest for rabbits or even birds, but you could not find anything. Now you sit in your canoe and stare hopefully into the clear water. If only you could spear a fish! It would not make a fine meal like the red deer, but it would stop the hunger pains.

Suddenly you see a large duck bobbing in the river. You have a bow and arrow. It has a sharpened flint tip fastened by a rope to a wooden shaft. You take aim and send the arrow into the air. You hit the duck! But the bird sinks quickly into the water. You scramble after it, but before you get there it is lost. What terrible luck!

It is growing dark and cold as you set out for home, empty-handed. You cannot face the hungry eyes of your children. Then, suddenly, you hear something squeal. A wild pig is caught in some brambles. You kill it swiftly with your spear.

You let out a wild cry of joy. Tonight your family will eat after all. But wait! Is that a yelp? What makes that sound? You go to a half-rotten stump and find three wolf pups in a nest. Two are already dead. The adult wolves must have been killed. Now the pup that still lives yelps and stares at you. A smile comes to your face.

Wouldn't it be something to not only bring home a nice fat pig to be roasted, but a wolf pup as well? What smiles would come to the faces of your children! The pup would make a merry companion for your youngsters.

But what then? The pup will grow into an adult wolf and then it will be dangerous. You will have to kill it and your children will be sad.

■ *If you take the pup home, turn to page 23.*

■ *If not, turn to page 24.*

Find out what your fate is!

You pick up the pup and it nips at your fingers. "You are hungry too, eh?" you mumble. The pup is half grown. He will eat your leftovers.

Your children scream with delight when you walk into the cave. The sight of the squirming ball of fur makes them happier than the thought of a full stomach tonight. You laugh and roast the wild pig over the fire. It is a good night. You will not go to sleep with hunger gnawing at your stomach.

In the days that follow, your children play tug-of-war with the wolf pup. They throw sticks for the pup to chase.

"Soon he will grow up and be dangerous," your spouse says. "Then we cannot keep him."

Your children look sad when they hear that. The oldest girl says, "Maybe this wolf will never be dangerous. He is one of our family. He likes us very much."

"All wolves are dangerous when they are grown," you say.

The wolf grows swiftly. He eats the scraps of bones from your hunting and fishing trips.

One day, as you go out to fish, the wolf follows you. He is beside you as you stand at the river and bait your line. You put a bit of fat on the hook and weight it down with a stone. Then you let it sink into the water. Soon a fish takes the bait. You jerk the line up quickly and admire the fine, fat fish. How delicious it will be when you roast it.

But before you can take the fish off the hook, the wolf snatches it.

"No!" you scream. You are filled with rage. You have little enough food without being robbed by this ungrateful beast you have raised. You snatch up a stick and hurl it at the wolf. He has already eaten the fish. Now he yelps and crawls into the brush. But he watches you from a distance.

You catch three more fish. Then you start for home. You will tell the children that the bad wolf ran away. But the wolf follows you! You would be lucky to be rid of the thieving beast. He is too big to keep anyway. Or should you give him another chance? Perhaps he did not mean to take the fish.

■ ***If you give the wolf another chance, turn to page 25.***

■ ***If not, turn to page 26.***

You ignore the wolf pup and go on your way. The pup would amuse your children, but then it would grow big and cause trouble. It could kill you or your children. And how would you feed it? You have enough just to keep your family fed.

You hurry home with the wild pig. You go into your cave and soon the pig is roasting. A wonderful smell fills the cave. Your children smack their lips and smile. Soon you eat roast pig, honey, and nuts. Everybody gets to eat their fill. But the pig is rather small. It will not last long. Tomorrow you must search for a deer. A deer will last longer.

As you sit by your fire in the cave, you see wolves in the darkness beyond the glow of your flames. The eyes of the wolves glow, too. They smell the pig meat. They want to share your kill.

You pick up stones and hurl them at the wolves, driving them back. They are still out there. But you cannot see them anymore.

"Wolves," you mutter.

"Very bad," says your spouse. "When I was small wolves killed my father."

The next day you go hunting early. When you get to a clearing you hear human voices. You do not know the hunters. Most people you meet are strangers. Your life is a lonely one. You draw back into the cover of the trees and watch. You can never be sure what will happen when you meet a stranger. There could be a violent fight. You could be injured or killed.

You watch the two hunters. They have a tame wolf! The wolf has helped them corner a large deer. You are amazed at how the wolf acts. He is almost like a third hunter. What a wonder!

The deer is swiftly killed. You stare at it hungrily. Would the hunters give you a portion of the meat if you traded a spearhead or an animal skin? Or if you went near them, would they become violent? They are very big and ferocious-looking.

■ ***If you approach the hunters, turn to page 27.***

■ ***If not, turn to page 28.***

You decide to let the wolf follow you. Maybe he will be useful to you.

As time goes by, the wolf becomes your constant companion. One morning he smells elk and you follow him to a meadow. You kill a large elk. You can feed your family for a long time with the meat. You make robes from the elk's skin to keep warm. Even the antlers are useful—you make new tools from them.

"The wolf is good," you tell your spouse.

Your spouse smiles and nods. It is safer at night in the cave when the wolf is here. He will growl and bark in warning when any stranger or other animal comes near.

All the wolf wants is scrap meat after you are finished eating. He lies happily by the fire.

One day when you are fishing, you spear a large duck. The wolf pulls the duck from the water and brings it to you. He drops it in the grass at your feet. He does not try to eat it. How clever and good the wolf has become!

"The wolf is a fine helper," you tell your daughter. "He helps me hunt."

Little by little, the wolf becomes more than a useful helper in the hunt. He becomes more than a protector who warns your family of danger near the cave. The wolf becomes something else.

Sometimes you sit by the fire and speak to the wolf. The wolf does not talk back, of course, but you see understanding in his eyes. The wolf knows you. The wolf likes being with you. You like the wolf, too.

The wolf is my friend, you think to yourself. He depends on you and you depend on him. You are very glad you took the wolf pup home that day. You are glad you gave the wolf a second chance.

As you walk with the wolf beside you, you realize that the wolf is a very special friend. He is never angry at you. He forgives you when you are angry with him (which is not often). In many ways the wolf is your very best friend.

■ ***Turn to page 29.***

You decide you cannot trust the wolf. You hurl stones at him until he stops following you. Then you go home with your fish.

"Where is the wolf?" your daughter says.

"The bad wolf stole my fish and then ran away," you say. "We are better off without a wild wolf."

Your daughter and two sons look very sad. They liked the wolf.

The next day you search for the herd of deer you have seen around here in the past. It is harder and harder to find game.

You climb a tall tree and look around. At last you see the herd, but it is in a faraway meadow. You scamper down the tree and run towards the meadow where you saw the herd. You hope you get there before they move.

When you reach the meadow you see a small deer near the edge of the herd, standing apart from the others. This one may be easier to kill. You hurl your spear—and miss! Oh no! Now the herd is on the run, scampering up the hills beyond your reach.

It is dusk already. You must bring something home for your hungry family to eat. The three fish you caught lasted but a day. You return to the river and fish. After a few minutes you catch a small fish. It will only be a mouthful for one person! You catch two more small fish before dark.

That night you sit by your fire with hunger pains growling in your stomach. You and your spouse had only a bite of the roasted fish. You gave the rest to the children. Even the children cannot eat their fill when there is so little meat. You have a few nuts to complete the meager meal.

But what hurts the most is what your daughter says: "I miss the wolf. The wolf was our friend."

You look into the fire and feel sorry that you drove the wolf away. Maybe one day you will find another wolf pup. It will all be different then. You will have more patience.

■ ***Turn to page 29.***

You walk slowly down into the meadow. You must not alarm the hunters. You don't want them to attack you. You grunt out a friendly greeting.

But the hunters think you have come to steal their kill. They do not give you a chance to explain. They scream at you and come after you with spears.

You raise your own spear in self-defense, but the biggest of the two hunters wounds you in the leg. You sink to the earth and pretend you are dead.

You lie very still as the hunters drag their kill away. They mount it on a pole and soon they are gone. Now, at last, you can moan. You did not dare make a sound while the hunters were here for fear they would strike you again.

Can you get home before you bleed to death? Your spouse is clever at healing wounds, but the pain is terrible. You are growing weaker by the moment. If you cannot reach home quickly, you will have no use of your spouse's healing herbs.

Suddenly, as you limp along, you notice a wolf running beside you in the brush.

You try to run faster. If you could only make it home! Once you fall, the wolf will be upon you!

Your legs are growing heavier. You stumble and get up again. You look beside you and see another wolf! You raise your spear with all your strength and drive it into the throat of the nearest wolf. The beast falls and the other one skulks away in fear.

Your cave is within sight. You drop to your knees, shouting for help. Your spouse and children come running. They carry you into the cave and put you down on an animal skin. The world grows dark. You are sure this is the end.

In a day you awaken. Your wound has been bound and you feel better. You smell roasting meat. How can it be? You failed to bring home a kill. Your daughter and two sons smile at you. They look very proud.

"We killed seven rabbits," says your daughter. "Two were very large."

"Good. Very good," you say. You are glad to see the sun shining beyond the cave. You never thought you would see it again on this earth.

■ ***Turn to page 29.***

You are afraid to go down and confront the men. They may try to kill you before you have the chance to speak. Still, you watch in fascination how the wolf works with the men. The hunters and the wolf cornered the animal together. Now the wolf does not touch the meat. He waits patiently for his share.

Maybe you made a mistake by not taking that wolf pup. You too could have had a tame helper. Maybe you would now have a deer to take home to your family.

You trudge on, searching for food. At last you come across some wild berries in the brambles. A few wild berries would taste good, but they won't help your family's hunger. Still, you stop to gather them.

Then you see bees around a tree. Honey! You decide to climb the tree and get some honey. As you reach the hive you are attacked by dozens of angry bees! You try to fend them off, but you tumble from the tree. What bad luck! Now your leg is sprained. You can hardly walk. Bee-stung and miserable, you limp home.

For many days you cannot hunt. You and your family must make do with roots and insects. You catch a few lizards and birds, but your family grows thin and weak.

"I will soon hunt again and bring home good meat," you promise. You carve yourself a walking stick and limp into the woodland the first chance you get. Your children go with you.

You walk for a day, but then you must rest your aching leg.

"We will look for game," your daughter says.

"You will find nothing. You will just get lost," you say.

But the children go. They are gone for half the afternoon, but when they return they are carrying a deer on a stick.

"We all worked together," they tell you. "And we were lucky."

You are proud of your children. At last there will be meat in the cave.

■ ***Turn to page 29.***

The Cave Dog

The first animal tamed in cave times was the wolf or the jackal. These animals were ancestors of dogs. If you look at some dogs today you can see they still look something like wolves. Big dogs like the German shepherd look more like wolves than little dogs like poodles.

The sharp sense of smell and hearing in the dog family was a big help to hunters. These animals helped find game and warned of danger. They were also companions to people. The friendship of a faithful animal was a big help. Then, as now, a dog could be somebody's best friend.

True/False

______ 1. Around 8500 B.C. there were dugout canoes.

______ 2. Barbed spears were carved from deer antlers.

______ 3. The bear was the first animal tamed.

______ 4. Tamed wolves were a serious problem to human hunters in the cave times.

______ 5. The cave hunters sometimes speared fish or caught them with baited hooks.

Group Activities

1. From the food items mentioned in the various stories, make a menu for an ordinary cave meal.
2. Look at a large map and find where the sheet of ice in the Ice Age extended. Which parts of the world were covered with ice? Was the place where you live covered?
3. At night the cave people told stories to entertain themselves. Choose several volunteers to make up an exciting story to tell. Then vote on the most entertaining of the stories.

Individual Activities

1. Imagine you are a cave hunter who found a wolf pup that grew up to be a companion. Name the wolf, and write one paragraph describing his qualities.
2. Find pictures of tools commonly used in 8000 B.C., such as spearheads, needles, fishhooks, and flint axes. Draw pictures of them.
3. Make a model of one of the tools you have drawn.

The Surprising Sumerians—2400 B.C.

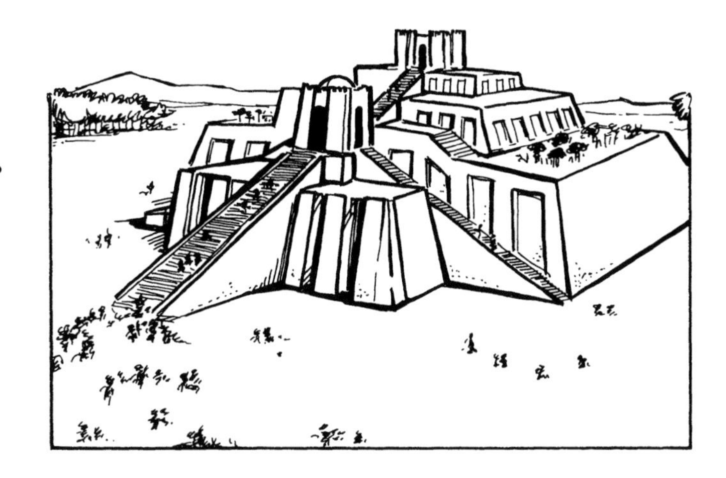

You are a skilled metalworker in the city of Lagash.[1] Before your time, people found nuggets of gold and copper and hammered them into the shapes they wanted. But now you have learned how to melt metal into liquid. You can make wonderful new things people never could make before.

You know how to mix tin with copper to make bronze. You make fine knives and axe heads. You also make great curved sickles, knives for cutting grain in the field. Workers swing the sickles and the grain falls. You also know how to make spearheads for soldiers.

Many people live on the Tigris and Euphrates rivers in Mesopotamia.[2] You can keep busy working all the time. You enjoy your work. It's a great joy to watch the liquid metal form useful shapes. There is such beauty in bronze.

Your skills at making weapons is very much needed now. There is a war going on against the state of Umma. You are young and don't understand all the issues in the war. You are sorry that so many people are dying.

Now you sit under a palm tree and think about your future. You would rather make bronze wine flagons than weapons. It makes you happy to think of these fine cups being used in times of joy and celebration. How many families will drink from them and feel warm and glad!

You often go to the ziggurat (religious temple) and admire the bronze decorations on the walls. You would feel so proud to make some of these lovely ornaments.

But you love Lagash, your city. It is your duty to help it in times of trouble. Perhaps you should make the sharp metal spears to be carried into battle.

■ ***If you make war materials, turn to page 33.***

■ ***If you make flagons and ornaments, turn to page 34.***

Find out what your fate is!

[1] In the Sumerian civilization

[2] Now Iraq

You decide to make spears for the soldiers.

"I am playing a part in helping my people," you proudly tell your father. You have always shared your feelings with your parents. As a child you would come home from school and recite your tablet to them.

Your father smiles now. He is a cattle breeder. He is very wealthy. "Yes, it is important that Umma be crushed. We have a good life here. I do not want it taken from us," he says.

You go to work making spearheads. When Umma is defeated you are called to the royal palace.

"Your swords played a big part in the victory," you are told. "Your blades won the day in a major battle. We cut off the heads of the Ummaites with ease! Already we have begun to make decorations describing the great victory."

You shudder at the story of the battle. But you are glad your side won. Now you go to work with other artists to make grand ornaments depicting the battle scenes. Sumerian children will see the decorations and feel pride in the great warriors of their land.

The artists make a large stone sculpture. It shows the Sumerian army advancing. It shows headless Ummaites lying there. Great vultures are carrying their heads away. You work on smaller bronze figures, warriors with gold helmets. Your art will last for thousands of years. You are proud of your figures of Sumerian warriors in war wagons holding spears and axes aloft.

Now, because so many resources were used up in the war, taxes must be raised.

"They are taking my cattle away from me to pay my taxes," groans your father. "I have worked all my life for what I have. Now I am losing it!"

The high taxes are harming your life's work, too. When you bring your bronze figures to the market to sell, the tax collector takes half of the money. He tells you, "The Sumerian ruler is in need of money."

In the marketplace the next day the tax collector comes again. He wants more. "I cannot give more!" you shout.

"You shall give me what I ask for," growls the tax collector in a threatening way. You must stop him from grabbing your figures! Or should you take them and run?

■ ***If you fight, turn to page 35.***

■ ***If you run, turn to page 36.***

You decide to make cups and ornaments and sell them in the marketplace. Many rich Sumerians want ornaments for their harps and as jewelry.

You hammer out the figure of a goat standing against a tree. It has a golden face, and fleece of lapis lazuli, a rich blue stone. This object is quickly bought by a wealthy farmer. Then you make a beautiful bronze bull's head as a harp decoration. Your bronze necklace has hanging pendants of hammered gold.

You are making a lot of money. Then you get a message from the king himself! You are to come to the palace at once. You are stunned. King Urukagina must have heard of your beautiful work.

"What an honor," says your father. "Go at once!"

You hurry to the palace. You wait in a large room. As you wait, an old woman talks to you. "What are you here for?" she asks.

"I am a bronze craftsperson and the king has called me," you boast. "I think he must have heard of my fine work. Perhaps he wants me to make ornaments for the palace. Perhaps a necklace for his wife."

The old woman nods. "You will become a servant of the ruler. You will be well treated. You will eat from the rich groves and gardens and never want for anything."

You smile. It all sounds very nice.

"Your feasts will flow with fat and milk, and there will be merriment as long as the ruler lives," says the old woman.

You don't like the sly smile that has come to the old woman's face. She seems to think being a royal servant has its bad side, too. What does she mean, "as long as the ruler lives"? Does something awful happen to the king's servants if he dies?

Fear grips you. You know little of such things. Perhaps you ought to pretend you are ill and just slip away. Perhaps you should tell a servant that you suffer from a severe sickness and cannot meet the king. Surely you would be forgiven for that.

Or are you letting the old woman deprive you of a wonderful job in the royal palace?

■ ***If you leave, turn to page 37.***

■ ***If you remain to meet the ruler, turn to page 38.***

You grab the tax collector and push him away. Soon you are both rolling and kicking in the street. Your nostrils fill with dirt. Great clouds of dust swirl around the battle. Then the tax collector strikes a terrible blow, almost crushing your shoulder. You lie bleeding in the street as he snatches up almost all your ornaments and goes off with them.

You drag yourself to the nearest physician for help.

"Ah, you have been fighting," says the doctor, shaking his head.

"I was set upon by a thieving tax collector," you groan. What a terrible pain the bleeding wound sends all through your arm and neck!

The physician stops the blood with a poultice. The shelves of his room are lined with many remedies. He uses milk, snakeskins, and powdered turtle shells. Most of his medicine comes from plants, though. Now he pounds an herb into fine dust and mixes it with water and honey. He gives it to you in a cup. "Drink all of this," he says.

You drink the mixture down. It doesn't taste too bad. It's sweet and a little comforting. But you wonder if the fellow knows what he's doing. You hope so. Your uncle died from a serious wound similar to yours.

Luckily, your wound heals, but for a long time you cannot work at your trade. Your arm is very weak. Your fingers are numb.

One day you hear some very good news. The ruler of Lagash has been thrown out. A new, fairer ruler has taken over. Now the tax collector will not always be at the throats of the people!

You begin to work on a new ornament. You make a wooden model first. Then you hammer thin plates of copper over it. You have made a beautiful bull's head. You smile in delight. You are still an artist! The wound did not destroy your gift! You can now make a good living again at your craft. Best of all, nothing makes you happier than your work. You are very grateful for that.

■ ***Turn to page 39.***

You snatch up your figures and run from the tax collector. You sprint through the crowded marketplace. You scatter baskets of chickens and fruit. People scream in rage after you. But you still have your beautiful ornaments and you got away from the greedy tax collector.

But where in Sumer can an honest craftsperson hide from the tax collectors?

You go to your father's house for advice. "What should I do?" you ask.

"We must have a new ruler in Sumer," says your father.

"But our ruler represents our god," you say.

"Only when he rules fairly. He was chosen by us—the free people of Lagash," your father storms. "We shall gather together and demand a more just ruler."

Your father and other men of his age hold meetings and plot against the ruler. After a while the rebellion succeeds. A new ruler comes to Lagash.

What a wonderful change you see! The tax collectors do not steal your father's cattle anymore. They don't steal half your ornaments. You can sell at the marketplace without being threatened.

New, fairer rules are put into effect in your land. Poor men have as much to say as rich men. Criminals are driven from town. Lagash is cleared of thieves and murderers.

You are very pleased with the new ruler. Soon you marry and have children. You send your children off to school every day. You give them each two rolls of bread for lunch, for a hungry child cannot learn well.

You want your children to do their schoolwork well every day so that when they grow up they will have a good life. They might choose to be teachers or physicians, or perhaps craftspeople, like you. Whatever they choose, you hope they are as happy at work as you are.

■ ***Turn to page 39.***

Pleading illness, you hurry off. The old woman has frightened you! You tell the servants of the ruler that you must tend to your sickness and they promise to make your excuse for you. But you worry that the ruler may be angry at you anyway. You decide to leave Lagash and go to another city where you are not known.

When you arrive in Nippur, another Mesopotamian city, you begin at once making copper and bronze ornaments. You sell them in the marketplace.

One day you meet a very frightened woman. "My husband was murdered a week ago," she tells you. "Bad men came in and killed him."

"Oh, how terrible. Have you reported the crime?" you ask.

"I am afraid to! If I tell what the murderers did to my husband they may come back and kill me, too," says the woman.

"But you must tell. Otherwise the murderers will escape punishment," you say.

Soon after you have spoken with the woman, the three men who killed her husband are arrested. But the poor woman is arrested too! "Why are you arresting this woman?" you ask. You feel very sorry for her.

"Ah," says a guard. "One of the murderers says she knew of the crime and covered it up for them. So she is also guilty."

How unfair that seems to be. The woman is only scared. How can someone be punished for being scared?

There is a trial in Nippur. You go to see what happens. Your father taught you that there is justice in the world. Now you wonder.

Nine men will decide what will be done with the three murderers and the woman who kept quiet. They listen to everyone's story, then they discuss it among themselves. Now one of the nine men stands to give the decision.

"They who killed the man may not live anymore. And the woman who hid the death of her husband must also die."

"But what crime did the woman commit?" you cry, along with others in the assembly.

The nine judges talk among themselves again. Then one of them speaks. "She did not kill her husband. She just kept quiet. So it will be enough to kill the three men who committed the murder. The woman will go free."

You are glad the woman was spared. You are pleased that justice was done after all.

■ ***Turn to page 39.***

The ruler asks you into his beautiful chambers. It is just as you thought it would be. He has heard of your artistic skill as a metalworker.

"You shall be the royal metalworker—an attendant of your ruler," he says.

You bow down gratefully. From now on you work only for the ruler and his royal court. You make gold and silver headdresses for the women of the court. You adorn the royal harps with golden goats and the copper heads of bulls. It's a splendid life.

The great feasts are marvelous. You eat from plates heaped with roasted venison and glowing fruit from the royal orchards. Green grapes, bursting with sweet juice, almost melt in your mouth. You travel with the ruler and his family as they hunt lions in the mountains. Then you make bronze figures of the ruler's triumphs over the wild animals.

Then one day it all ends. A strange fever comes over the land. The ruler and his wife die within a week.

"Now we shall all die," says one of the servants.

At first you think the servant fears that you may all catch the fever that killed the royal family. But then you find out what it really means. When the ruler dies his servants must all be killed, so that all may be buried together.

You and all who served the ruler must walk down to the death pit. You walk downstairs into a deep mine. You enter a stone chamber. There are the dead ruler and his wife lying side by side. They are wearing much gold and jewelry. Some of it was made by your hands. The stone chamber is filled with golden cups and beautiful pottery. Even some of the ruler's soldiers are here to die so they might be buried with him.

You must drink the poison that is given to you. You are young. You don't want to die. But you have no choice. Your ruler is dead, so you must die, too. You grow dizzy and you quickly lie down in a row next to a dying soldier. Soon you are dead.

The pit is filled up with tons of earth. It will be many thousands of years before this place is discovered. Your remains will be found among 120 servants who died this day in Sumer.

■ ***Turn to page 39.***

School Days in Sumer

In Sumer children went to school every day. When the student misbehaved he was caned (hit with a stick). Lessons were written on clay tablets. The clay was soft. Reeds were used as pens. Sumerians didn't use letters; they used symbols. The written language of Sumer was called *cuneiform.* It looked like little wedges hitched together in all kinds of different ways.

The children sat on benches made of baked brick. They studied arithmetic, animals and plants, and stories of the history of Sumer.

Not every child in Sumer went to school, though. Most of the students came from rich families. The poor could not afford to go. And we are pretty sure the students were all boys.

Matching

______	1. Mixing tin and copper produced	a) ziggurats
______	2. The pens Sumerian children used were	b) flagons
______	3. The religious temples were called	c) bronze
______	4. A major city in the Sumerian civilization was	d) Lagash
______	5. Bronze wine cups were called	e) reeds

Group Activities

1. Using history reference books and encyclopedias, copy the cuneiform words for ten common objects and make a large poster of them.
2. The temple of Sumer was a ziggurat. Find a picture of one and draw it. Conduct an art contest over who has drawn the most realistic, most colorful, most imaginative ziggurat.
3. How was Sumerian school life different from school life now? Discuss what it was probably like to be a student in Sumer.

Individual Activities

1. Find the Tigris and Euphrates rivers on a modern map. What countries do they run through today? Write them down.
2. Make a small square of clay and make a wedge-shaped writing instrument out of wood. Press your writing instrument into the clay to form "cuneiform" symbols. Notice how easy they are to erase to make a new space to write.
3. When Sumerians died they often left behind stone statues of themselves. These statues were then placed at the temples. Find pictures of these statues and sketch them. The statues often had big, round, blue eyes.

Babylon and Beyond—1800 B.C.

You are a young Babylonian and your king is Hammurabi. He is a fair lawgiver and you respect him. You live here on the middle Euphrates and you are very proud of your clean and orderly streets. They are lined with houses and workshops. Your father is an official of the king. Your mother wears long, flounced skirts and she has a mind of her own on just about everything.

"This Hammurabi has laws that are good for women as well as men," says your mother. "If a man leaves his wife, he must continue to support her."

Hammurabi's laws make a lot of sense to everybody. But some are very stern. Hammurabi says that if a son strikes his father, then the son's hands must be cut off. If a builder makes a mistake on a house and it falls down and kills the person living there, the builder must be killed.

You must plan what to do in life. You surely don't want to be a builder! You would be killed if your house fell down on the owner.

"If you become a doctor," says your father, "and kill your patient by mistake, then your hands will be cut off."

You didn't want to be a doctor anyway.

You would really like to be a merchant. There are stern laws for merchants, too. You must never cheat anybody. But you wouldn't do that anyway. You are an honest person.

"I could travel and see interesting places. I could bring pearls and ivory from India if I traveled to the islands off Arabia," you say.

"Or you might sell our beautiful cloth to the towns in the north," your father says.

"Ah," says your mother. "You will need a loan to get started. You must buy products to trade for. I have my own money. I will make you a loan."

You thank your mother for her kind offer. You will take her up on it.

Now you must decide to go south to Arabia or north to the towns along the road.

■ ***If you go south, turn to page 43.***

■ ***If you go north, turn to page 44.***

Find out what your fate is!

You make a voyage to the islands off Arabia with clothing, silver, and vegetable oils. You land on Telmun Island[1] in the Persian Gulf. You hope to trade your goods for copper, pearls, and ivory, which have been brought here from the Indus Valley of India.

Once you land on the island you load your goods on donkeys and head for the marketplace. You hope to make a very good profit. If you do, you will buy some land for your future. When you are weary of the life of a merchant you will sit under a tree and watch your vineyards grow in Babylon.

You see a fellow coming in the opposite direction. He gives you a hearty smile and shouts, "Ah, a trader from Ur.[2] What are you taking to the marketplace?"

"Fine clothing and silver and oils," you say.

"It is such a long and tiresome journey to the marketplace," says the man. "Let us make a deal right here."

"What do you have to trade?" you ask. "I see no donkeys laden with goods following you, my friend."

The man smiles again and brings down a small sack from this shoulder. "I have a very small object. It is not as heavy as your cloth, silver, and oils, but it is worth far more. If I exchanged this treasure for the goods on all your donkeys you would have the best part of the bargain."

You are really curious now. "Let me see this treasure at once!"

"Ah." The man opens his sack to reveal a gold necklace. "This was intended for a royal lady. It is worth a fortune. Take it in exchange for all your goods and we shall go our separate ways."

"Why would you part with such a treasure?" you ask.

"Because I am afraid to carry it. What if I am knocked down and robbed? I am too old to fight off robbers, while you are young and strong."

You wonder where the treasure came from. Is it stolen? You know you will not get the truth by asking. But you also know that the necklace is truly worth all the goods you brought from Babylon.

■ ***If you make the trade, turn to page 45.***

■ ***If not, turn to page 46.***

---

[1] Now Bahrain

[2] City in Babylon

You load donkeys with clothing and begin the long journey to the northern towns. You carry beautiful garments for women and fine clothing for men. Your mother looked over the clothing and assured you it was the best. You are especially proud of the long, full skirts you carry. They are richly embroidered, as are the robes and cloaks for men.

You arrive at a bustling marketplace. Soon people gather to look at your clothing. A pretty young woman comes forward and says, "Ah, merchant, I have need of skirts such as those."

Well, the young woman looks very poor indeed. The skirt she is wearing is full of holes! How could such a woman pay you the price these skirts must bring? "My dear lady, I took this clothing from a shopkeeper in Ur," you tell her. "I must bring back silver for it. If I fail to get a just price I will bring trouble on my own head and I will make no profit for myself. Hammurabi has said that a merchant who has not sold goods for a just price must pay back the shopkeeper double the value."

"But what of showing mercy to a poor woman like me?" she says. "As you can see, I have great need of a new skirt. My skirt is falling off for wear. Would you deprive me of clothing for lack of silver? Have mercy and take in trade some barley I have. I know it is not a fair trade, but Hammurabi urges mercy, too."

You don't know what to do. You do feel sorry for the young woman. And you have many skirts. If you sold one for a poor price, you might be able to make it up on other sales. There are very wealthy-looking people in the marketplace today. Surely many of them will purchase your beautifully embroidered clothing.

Still, you must bring back to the shopkeeper the right amount of silver or you will be accused of cheating him. You might be ruined as a merchant before you have even started your career!

■ ***If you trade the skirt for barley, turn to page 47.***

■ ***If not, turn to page 48.***

You grasp the necklace. It glitters in the sunlight. It is the most beautiful thing you have ever seen! The gold of the necklace is in the shape of beech and willow leaves. It does indeed seem like a rare treasure. You gladly give the man your laden donkeys and he hurries off with them.

As you turn and head back to the ship that brought you here, you are thrilled by your good fortune. You only spent a few hours on the island and you made an excellent deal.

You are almost to the seacoast when you are overtaken by two angry-looking men.

"There is the thief!" cries one.

You cannot believe they mean you, but they do.

"I am no thief," you insist.

The men seize you roughly and search you, finding the necklace at once. "Aha!" shouts the bigger of the two. "Here it is!"

"But I did not steal that. I traded it with an old man on the road. I thought he had come by it honestly. I gave him my donkeys laden with goods in exchange. I stole nothing," you say.

You are bound and dragged off. One of the men says to you, "This was stolen from a temple. You know the law of Hammurabi. If one has stolen from a temple that one shall be put to death."

"But I did not steal from a temple!"

"The law of Hammurabi says that if one has received stolen property that one should be put to death," says the big fellow.

"Wait," you say. "It is Hammurabi's law that if you receive stolen property without knowing it is stolen then you are innocent!"

"Do you have witnesses to the trade you say took place?" asks the smaller of the two men.

You are terror-stricken. Only the old man knows the truth. Even if he should be found, of course he would deny everything. Otherwise he would doom himself—for he must be the real thief.

You are swiftly executed for a crime you did not commit.

■ ***Turn to page 49.***

"I believe I will take my goods on to the marketplace," you say. You fear the necklace is stolen. The law code of Hammurabi orders death to one who receives stolen goods.

The man mutters to himself and hurries on.

When you reach the marketplace, you carefully examine the copper, pearls, and ivory. You are a clever trader. You will only accept good quality. The other trader looks at your silver and clothing and vegetable oils. You can see he also is clever. You will argue a long time before a deal is made. But that is all right. That is what being a good merchant is. Eventually you strike a good bargain. Then you sit down under an acacia tree and talk as friends.

"What news have you of the Indus Valley?" you ask.

"We have delightful toys and beautiful floral pottery. When you come again perhaps you would like to see these as well," he says.

"Yes. Is life pleasant there?" you ask. You like to find out about other places in the world.

The man smiles. "We have fine bazaars. One can buy anything. How is your life in Ur? Is Hammurabi truly a just man?" he asks.

"Yes, he is. Our life is good. But the prices are too high," you say.

You finish a small lunch and head for the seacoast. It takes many hours to load all your new goods into the bull boat. The boat is a large, circular basket, woven and covered with hides, that is big enough to carry you, your donkeys, and your goods. You paddle north from the island toward home. When you get your goods to the opposite shore you will break up the boat, load the donkeys, and return home.

You are welcomed by the shopkeepers whose goods you traded. Your profit is a handsome one. You are well launched on your career. On your next journey you are gone for almost two years, and you come back with apes, ivory, and colorful peacocks. You are getting rich, and your future is bright indeed.

■ ***Turn to page 49.***

You give the woman the skirt and take the barley in exchange. You will make it up somehow.

"Oh, the blessings of the gods on you. May your wealth be great. May your family always enjoy good health."

"Thank you, good woman," you say.

As you sell your other goods, a man comes over. He is well dressed. You can tell he is a patrician, a nobleman from the rich class. "I have been watching you," he says. "For a young trader you are very sharp. You make good bargains, but you are honest. I would like you to sell my goods for me. But one thing troubles me."

"What is that?" you ask.

"I saw you almost give away a richly embroidered skirt to a poor woman. Did I see it correctly? Do you willingly make such a foolish bargain as that?"

You do not want to appear to be a fool, but you are honest. You must tell the truth.

"I did take pity on that woman," you say. "I believe in kindness and mercy. To be so greedy that there is no place in your life for mercy is not a good thing. Have you heard the fable of the nine wolves and the tenth one?"

"No," admits the man. "I have not heard the fable, but I will listen to it now if you wish me to."

"Well," you begin, "there were ten wolves in a meadow and they killed ten sheep. The tenth wolf was greedy. He said, 'I will take for myself nine sheep to eat. The other nine of you can eat the tenth sheep.' Would you have me be so greedy as that bad wolf?"

The man laughs heartily. "You are clever in word and deed. I would like you to trade for me."

You grin. You are glad you are clever with words. When you went to school your teachers warned you that you must listen carefully in order to be wise. You listened. And now you are using your wisdom to good effect.

■ ***Turn to page 49.***

"All my goods must bring a fair price," you say. "I am sorry you lack a decent skirt, but this is not my fault."

The woman goes away sad. Just then another trader walks up. "I saw what just happened. You are a good trader. You are not moved by pity to do foolish things."

"I must do right by the shopkeepers whose goods I carry," you say.

"There is no room for pity in the heart of a merchant, eh?" asks the other trader.

You shake your head. It is too bad this is so, but it is. By nightfall you have sold all your goods at very just prices. But then, as you are gathering your silver, you are robbed! Three burly fellows beat you badly and steal all your silver.

You crawl down the dirt road, crying for help. "I have been robbed!" you shout.

A craftsperson sees you and says, "Oh, what a sad thing. A thief has beaten and robbed you. I wish I could help you, but I must get to my workplace and make a coat."

A scribe comes along then. You beg him for help.

"Pitiful fellow, I wish I could help you, but you see, an important person waits for me. But I wish you luck," he says before hurrying on.

Then you see the trader you met before. How thankful you are! Surely a fellow trader will help you.

"Help! I have been beaten and robbed," you groan.

"Oh, what miserable luck," he says. "It is a cruel and heartless world, my friend. I must make a deal this night or I would stop and take you to my own home to bind your wounds. Ah, there is no room for pity in the heart of a merchant . . ." Then he vanishes in the darkness.

You try to stem the blood from your wounds. How will you explain to the shopkeepers of Ur that you have lost their goods and the silver?

You hope *they* will have pity.

■ ***Turn to page 49.***

Long-Ago Toys

Stone Age children played with seeds in gourds. They shook them and enjoyed the sound just as babies today enjoy rattles. Later on children played with clay and wooden balls. In Egypt children had tiny cooking utensils and they pretended they were grown-ups with these toys. Asian children in prehistoric times had kites.

Hero, a scientist who lived in 100 B.C. in Alexandria, Greece, made very detailed toys. He made a singing bird and tiny moving figures. The Aztecs of Mexico made little wheeled pull toys for their children. Even long, long ago, parents wanted to give their children toys to make them happy.

Matching

______	1. The lawgiver of Babylon	a) India
______	2. Where Hero was from	b) kites
______	3. Pearls and ivory came from	c) Hammurabi
______	4. Little wheeled pull toys were used by	d) Alexandria
______	5. Asian children sometimes played with	e) Aztecs

Group Activities

1. Get a copy of the law code of Hammurabi. Choose ten of the laws. Write them on the board and discuss their fairness.
2. Make small bull boats, using piano wire or sandwich ties to make the circular frame. You can get a round shape by molding the wire around a bowl. Tape brown paper on the frame to look like hides. Put a stick in either side for the oars.
3. Make a poster of Babylonian art. Copy the figures shown on the mosaic panels of the Royal Standard of Ur. You can find a picture of it in most encyclopedias under *Art of the Ancient World*, or on page 53 of the book *The Last Two Million Years* (see Bibliography).

Individual Activities

1. In one paragraph give your opinion of the law code of Hammurabi.
2. Find the city of Ur and Telmun (Bahrain) on the map.
3. In one paragraph describe a way the law code of Hammurabi affected women.

Indus Valley Decision—1700 B.C.

You live in the town of Mohenjo-Daro in the Indus Valley. Your father and mother grow wheat, barley, peas, melons, and dates. You also have a fine herd of sheep and goats. A huge granary on the river holds excess grain from your fields, so that in bad years you don't go hungry.

Right now your mother is carrying your younger brother outside. He is five.

"You must amuse him," your mother tells you. "I have to do my chores now."

Your house is made of wood and brick. Because it is so hot here, the flat roof is covered with clay. There are date trees near the house. They provide shade from the hot sun. You take your small brother under a date tree. "Here," you say, "play with your little donkey cart." Your brother has a tiny toy donkey whose head bobs up and down when he pulls it along. He also has small clay dogs, elephants, and pigs to play with.

"Play with me," insists your brother. You have games of jacks, marbles, and dice. But you don't feel like playing now.

"Here's our dog," you say as the family pet comes runnning. "He will play with you."

Soon your little brother is amused by the dog. You decide to do some exploring this morning. You run down to the great bazaar in town. There are so many interesting sights there. The stalls are packed tightly together and form high walls and alleys. You love to look in all the stalls and see new things.

When you reach the bazaar you see a long passage which is decorated with red and black paintings. Elsewhere, there are bright blue swimming pools.

On such a hot morning the swimming pools look delightful. Is the water cool? You are tempted to dip your finger in and see. But maybe it is not permitted. You smell a new perfume from the long passage. Is that a new fruit you have not tasted before?

■ *If you go down the passage, turn to page 53.*

■ *If you go closer to the swimming pools, turn to page 54.*

Find out what your fate is!

You hurry down the long passageway looking for the source of the fragrance. You stop and stare at a stone bust, a statue of head and shoulders. The bust is of a bearded man with narrow, slitted eyes. He looks very stern. You run along, but suddenly your way is blocked by two tall, fierce-looking men. They look like ruffians!

You run between the men toward a group of merchants just ahead. A lamb bleats as you go by. You dare not look around to see if the men are chasing you. Then, at last, you sit down under a date tree to catch your breath. Nobody is following you now. You are tired, hot, and hungry. And you are far from home.

You are lost!

There is a saying here that the sun can kill. You must get home, but you cannot wander around in the hot sun. The streets all look strange. You have never been here before.

You have heard of dangerous bandits who live in the mountains. They live off the land, hunting wild animals. Sometimes they come down and rob people. You must not fall into the hands of a roaming bandit.

You walk slowly, trying to stay under the shade of trees. Oh, it is so hot today! If only you were home under the date tree. Soon your mother would call you to eat.

You see a group of people ahead. They look like artisans or traders. The men have beards but they have shaved upper lips. Their long hair is gathered in buns at the back of their heads. They wear kilts and shawls.

You wonder if you should go to these men and ask for help. Or could you find your way home by yourself? You don't know these men. They are strangers. You don't even know what kind of people they are.

■ ***If you try to go home by yourself, turn to page 55.***

■ ***If you ask for help, turn to page 56.***

You go to the swimming pool nearest you. How refreshing it would be to jump in! It is growing hotter by the minute. When you rise in the morning it is already hot, but then it keeps getting hotter and hotter.

You kneel by the side of the pool and dip your finger in.

"The pool is for religious ceremonies only," says the stern voice of a man behind you.

You scramble away from the pool area. You hurry to the bazaar. A monkey chatters from the shoulder of a trader.

"Oh," you cry in delight, "is that monkey for sale?"

"Yes," says the trader, "and a fine pet it is. Do you have a dog?"

"Yes, we have a dog."

"Well, the monkey is a better pet. But he will get along well with the dog. Do you have a cat?" asks the trader.

"Oh yes, we have a cat. Sometimes the dog and the cat fight."

"Ah, the monkey is a better pet. But he will not fight with the dog or the cat," says the trader.

You stare at the monkey. What a wise little face he has. He seems to like you right away. He stares at you through his pretty, dark-brown eyes. You want him very much. But what have you got to trade for such a fine monkey?

"Wait here, sir," you say. You run home as fast as you can. You must beg your mother to give you something to trade for the clever little monkey.

But when you get home, your mother and your little brother are away visiting neighbors. You must make the decision yourself.

You see one of your mother's jars. It is quite pretty, with black figures on a red field. It has a shiny finish. Your mother has several such jars. She would surely not mind if you traded one for the monkey. But perhaps she *would* mind, because she loves pretty things.

You go outside and see a fine young goat. The trader would like her. But should you trade away a fine young goat that will give milk when she is grown?

■ ***If you take the vase, turn to page 57.***

■ ***If you take the goat, turn to page 58.***

You try to find your own way home. You look around for a familiar landmark. You walk for a long time before you see a huge banyan tree. Its roots grow down from the branches. There are hundreds of dangling roots. Each will go into the ground and become another trunk. The tree already has one thousand trunks.

"Ah," you cry out. "I have seen that big banyan tree before. Now I know which direction to take." You walk faster. Then you run.

You see farmers ploughing their fields with water buffalo. You wave to those you know. You are very near home now. How glad you are! For a while there, you were afraid, but you won't admit that to anybody.

Suddenly you see a tiger in the path ahead. The tiger is hiding in a clump of brush. He has come out of the nearby thick jungle. All your life you have feared man-eating tigers. Sometimes they eat young goats and lambs and even children!

You run for your life as the tiger comes after you in great, springing leaps. You catch hold of a low-hanging tree branch and swing up into the tree.

Tigers can climb trees, too. But this tiger looks old and heavy. You hope he decides not to come up after you. Your arm is scratched from your quick leap into the tree. You are hot and thirsty and miserable as the tiger prowls around the bottom of the tree. The tiger puts his paws on the trunk of the tree and snarls. He is very hungry too! He wants you for lunch!

In the distance you see the farmer you waved to before. He seems to be looking in your direction. You scream and wave your arms.

The farmer and his brothers come with fiery sticks and spears. The tiger does not wait long. He is gone in a streak back to the jungle.

You thank your neighbors very much. Then they scold you. "You must not roam all alone so far from home," says one of them.

You run the rest of the way home. The next time you go exploring you will be much more careful.

■ ***Turn to page 59.***

You approach a man wearing a large shawl.

"I am lost," you explain. You describe where you live.

"Ah, you must be very rich to live in so nice a place," says the man. He calls to another man and they ask you to follow them. But as you walk through a narrow hall, the two men turn and seize you! You are swiftly bound and gagged and put into a sack! You are loaded on a donkey. Soon you are heading for the mountains north of your village.

You are terrified. What will become of you?

Far up in the mountains you are dumped from the sack and untied. You are in the camp of a rough band of bandits. They live by robbing the trade caravans. The leader of the bandits grabs you by the shoulders and shouts in your face, "You will do the work you are told to do. You will take care of the animals. If you try to escape we will cut your throat!"

How could you try to escape when you don't even know the way home?

As the days go by you long to be home in your own nice house. You miss your parents and your little brother. You miss your pleasant, clean house. Here you must sleep on dirty animal skins and wash in a muddy creek. By the end of the first week you don't even look like yourself any more.

Little by little you forget your former life. You find friendship with two other captive children and they become your family. When you are older and stronger, the three of you escape. You join a band of nomadic cattle raisers. You travel with them from place to place.

Years later you return to your own home. Invaders have moved in and your family is gone. Nobody even knows what happened to them. The town you knew lies in ruins. You do not even look for your old home. It would just make you sadder.

You spend your life raising cattle in the hills. You try to look to the future. But often you think of beautiful Mohenjo-Daro.

■ ***Turn to page 59.***

You grasp the vase and carry it toward the bazaar. But, as you run, you stumble and fall. The vase flies from your hands and shatters on a stone.

"No!" you cry. You stoop and pick up the pieces. You must somehow put the vase back together. But the pieces are so small. It's just impossible.

Sadly you return home with the broken pieces. If you tell your parents you were taking the vase to trade for a monkey, they will be twice as angry. Now they have neither a vase nor a monkey. You must think of a good story to make them less angry.

As you reach your house, you see that your mother and brother have returned home.

"What have you there?" your mother asks.

"Oh, I have our poor broken vase," you say.

Your mother looks angry. "How did this happen? Why isn't the vase inside the house where it belongs?"

"Well," you say, "there was an earthquake while you were gone. I was afraid the vase might fall down and break. So I grabbed it and ran outside. But the earth was shaking so hard that I fell and dropped the vase."

Your mother glares at you. "We were visiting at a neighbor's house. If the earth had shaken here it would have trembled there as well. You took the vase away without asking and now you are lying about what happened."

You hang your head and decide to tell the truth. "I was at the bazaar and I saw the finest monkey in the whole world. I knew we must have that monkey. So I took the vase to trade for him. I dropped the vase on the way to the bazaar," you say. "I know you would have liked the monkey. I am very sorry I spoiled it all."

Your mother still looks angry. "I would never have allowed you to take my beautiful vase to trade for anything. Why would we want a monkey?" she asks.

"I have never seen such a wonderful monkey," you say. "It would have been a fine pet."

Your mother mutters something. Then she says, "You really would have brought a monkey into this house?" And she laughs a little.

You breathe a sigh of relief. Things are getting better.

■ ***Turn to page 59.***

You lead the young goat back to the bazaar. You are sure your parents would approve of this. The little monkey will amuse your young brother. Your mother will have more time to work. Perhaps the wise little monkey can even be trained to do simple household tasks.

"Here is a goat to trade for the monkey," you tell the trader.

The trader seems very pleased. "A very nice goat indeed!" he says, making the exchange quickly.

You walk off with the monkey in your arms. You can't wait to show him to your family.

As you near your house you see your little brother. He has tired of playing with the dog. He is now playing with his small donkey cart.

"Look!" you shout.

Your brother comes running to meet you. When he sees the monkey he is frightened. He turns and runs back inside the house and hides.

Your mother comes out then. "What frightened your brother?" she asks. She looks at the monkey. "Where did you get that?"

"I traded one of our young goats for this fine monkey," you say.

"You traded a good goat, one that will soon give rich milk, for a foolish monkey?"

"I thought you would like the monkey," you say.

When your father comes in, he agrees with your mother. "You should have asked for permission to make the trade," he says. "Take the monkey back to the bazaar and bring our goat home at once."

You feel very sad. But you head back to the bazaar. You will miss the little monkey. Already you like him.

But when you get there the trader is gone. Your goat is gone, too. There is no chance to exchange.

You look at the monkey. "I guess you belong to us now," you say. The little monkey grins. At least you think he is grinning; with a monkey you can never be sure.

■ ***Turn to page 59.***

The Secret Cities of India

Until 1922 everybody thought Indian civilization had begun around 1500 B.C. They thought people called Aryans had built India's first cities. Then archaeologists made an amazing discovery. They found another, much older, civilization: the great walled cities of Harappa and Mohenjo-Daro. Here were great palaces and towers. Here were water pipes and children's toys. The people lived a pleasant and advanced life from about 3300 B.C. to 1500 B.C. Then the civilization disappeared. The Aryans took over. Maybe the Aryans were the ones who destroyed these ancient cities.

Matching

______	1. One of the grains grown in the Indus Valley	a) Harappa
______	2. To keep houses cool, roofs were covered with	b) bazaar
______	3. One of India's ancient cities	c) clay
______	4. The people who came to India around 1500 B.C.	d) barley
		e) Aryans
______	5. Where traders' stalls could be found	

Group Activities

1. Discuss the lives the people of Mohenjo-Daro led. What would you have liked, or disliked, about living there?
2. On an ancient civilization map find where Mohenjo-Daro and Harappa stood. What cities stand there now?
3. Carved seals from Mohenjo-Daro have been found. These seals were used to stamp goods. Find samples of these seals and copy them on a large poster. (Check page 514 of Helen Gardner's *Art Through the Ages* or any encyclopedia under *Ancient Civilizations* or *Indus Valley*).

Individual Activities

1. When archaeologists found the old Indus civilization they found skeletons in the streets and on stairs. They found charred wood. In one or two paragraphs write what you think happened to these cities.
2. You are a child in the Indus Valley. What toy would you select for your smaller brother or sister? Explain in one paragraph.
3. Using simple materials like clay or wood, make a toy similar to those found in the Indus Valley.

Careers in Crete—1400 B.C.

You live on Crete, an island off Greece. Your home is in the beautiful city of Minos. Olive orchards and vineyards cover the pale green hills. Your island lies in the middle of sparkling clear blue water. You cannot imagine a more beautiful home.

You are a young person who belongs to the royal family, so your life is special. You have been to the great palace at Knossos, where the walls are covered with brilliant paintings of people and animals. The painting you remember best showed a young woman leaping over a bull.

"What kind of young people get to do that?" you asked your father when you saw the painting.

"Very foolish ones, I think," said your father. You were small then and he did not want you to jump over bulls in the fields.

But you did not forget the painting. You decided you would leap over bulls when you were old enough.

Now you are old enough. You would like to take part in the bull-leaping rituals. What a thrill it would be to join the teams of young men and women who spend their time somersaulting over a bull's horns.

But your mother thinks it's a terrible idea. Your mother wants you to develop your skills of painting pottery. You *are* an artist. Already you paint vases with detailed octopuses, fish, and birds.

You watch your mother styling her long, beautiful hair. How pretty she is. She is wearing a short-sleeved jacket and a white blouse. Her lounging pajamas are decorated with ruffles. She wears high-heeled strapped slippers. Today when she goes out she will wear her large, brightly-decorated hat. But first she will paint her lips red. Now she turns to you and smiles. "You are not still thinking of bull-leaping, are you?"

■ ***If you try bull-leaping, turn to page 63.***

■ ***If you devote your time to vase-painting, turn to page 64.***

Find out what your fate is!

You cannot bear to pass up the thrill of bull-leaping. You want to go to the open-air theater and perform before hundreds of people and show what you can do.

You train long and hard for the great moment. The wild bulls that are used for the ritual are caught with nets. They must not be harmed. They are used only for the ritual. All your life you have heard that the bull is a sacred animal. Honoring bulls can bring good luck. It might even prevent earthquakes.

The trick of bull-leaping is to meet the charging bull between its horns. You must catch hold of its horns. Then you swing up and vault over the bull's back. You must develop perfect timing. You must have great acrobatic skill. You are not armed, because no matter what happens, the bull cannot be hurt. But sometimes the bull-leaper is badly hurt.

Finally the day of the ritual arrives. You march into the arena with other young people. Your heart is racing with excitement. You see the mighty bull charging at you. Will you perform gracefully, or be gored by the bull's horns? Just in time you leap up and grab the horns. Over you go to safety. As you land on your feet, one of your partners steadies you. You are smiling joyfully.

Over and over you perform the ceremony. Great crowds admire you. How proud you are! Maybe some artist will do a wall painting of you leaping over a bull.

While you are talking about your triumph in the arena, your father tells you of another adventure you might have. A relative is planning a voyage to Egypt and North Africa. You could go along if you wanted to.

But you could also continue bull-leaping if you wanted to. You are so good at it. In Crete it is believed to be a good and brave activity for a young person like you.

■ ***If you go on the sea voyage, turn to page 65.***

■ ***If not, turn to page 66.***

You set to work on your painting. You try all kinds of finishes. Soon you have painted some beautiful vases. You paint flowers and shells and fish on your vases, because things that remind people of the sea are very popular here. Crete is surrounded by the sparkling Mediterranean Sea.

One day you meet another artist from northern Greece.

"I live to the north on a hilltop," your new friend says. "I live in Mycenae. You should see our amazing forts. Some of the stones weigh tons. And our palaces have dozens of rooms."

"I would like to see it," you say.

"Then journey north with me. We will make a sea voyage and then go by land until we reach my city. We have frescoes—wall paintings that are painted on wet, fresh plaster—that are prettier than the ones I've seen here. I can show you a rock-crystal bowl in the form of a duck that is the most beautiful art object I have ever seen!"

Your parents are not happy with your plan to go to Mycenae.

"Why are you so restless?" asks your mother. "There is enough here in Crete to interest anyone. You can hunt and sing and dance. There is always something going on."

"Yes, who could imagine a more pleasant life?" asks your father.

You agree that Crete is very beautiful and you enjoy living here. But your new friend is eager to show you the way of life in Mycenae. His sister is a weaver and his brothers are masons and carpenters.

"Our home is on a hill which is covered with olive groves. It is really quite beautiful," your friend says. "I think we raise the sweetest grapes on earth. And the seas are so clear. I can look down and see the fish at the very bottom!"

You are eager for a new adventure, but perhaps you should stay right here on Crete and work on your art. If you are to be a great artist you must dedicate yourself to your work.

■ ***If you go to Mycenae, turn to page 67.***

■ ***If you remain in Crete, turn to page 68.***

How thrilling it is to be leaving on a great ship with a large square sail. The bow and stern are high and sharply curved up. The ship is steered by oars. You look up at the wind thumping the sail.

You find an incredibly different world in Egypt from that which you know in Crete. Amenhotep III rules Egypt, and Egypt rules much of the world. A young Egyptian you meet is boastful of that. "None dare defy us," says the Egyptian. "And even better, it is good for people to be ruled by Egypt, for we rule wisely."

You go with the Egyptian to a house made of mud brick and white plaster. The shutters on the windows help keep out the hot sun. You enter the house and sit on a goose-down stuffed pillow. You enjoy freshly baked bread.

That night you sleep on a wicker bed in a wooden frame. It's a very clever way to sleep in such a hot country. The cool air can come from beneath you through the loosely woven wicker. You do not use a pillow; you rest your head on a wooden headrest. It is surprisingly comfortable.

Your uncle takes care of his business here while you wander about with a group of young Egyptian friends. You see beautiful goblets of translucent alabaster in the shapes of lotus flowers. It gives you many new ideas for your own vases.

But the most beautiful sights you see in Egypt are surely the pyramids. What massive limestone blocks! You cannot imagine how such places were built. There is nothing in Crete like them.

After almost three years of traveling with your uncle, you return home. Your heart and mind are filled with wondrous sights. You feel you have really matured as a person. You are now ready to work as an artist, using as inspiration many of the sights you have seen.

But when you sail to Crete you make a shocking discovery. A terrible disaster has struck in your absence. Minos has been destroyed by some violent incident—an earthquake or volcano? All you know is that your entire family is dead. Now looters roam around, poking amid the ruins of what was once a beautiful city.

You travel north to Mycenae to become an artist there. But you cry for Minos and the beautiful life you once knew.

■ ***Turn to page 69.***

You remain in Crete and train for the next time you will leap over a bull in the arena. You are practicing your somersaults when you hear a strange, rumbling sound. You stumble and fall to your knees.

What is happening? The very earth trembles!

"Earthquake!" screams a friend.

But this does not feel like an earthquake. It feel as if the earth is exploding around you.

The wall is tumbling down. You want to run, but your legs are numb. You barely get away in time. The wall has fallen on your friend.

You run out into the sunlight. To the north there is dark smoke pouring into the sky. It is coming from the direction of the island of Thera (Santorin).

As you hurry toward home to see if your family is all right, you see ash falling from the sky. It is coming down like rain. "Volcano!" you gasp.

When you reach home you find that most of your family has been killed. Your house caved in on them. Only your younger sister is still alive. She was outside when the house caved in.

You grab your sister's hand and run. But where are you running to? You don't know. You are sobbing and running.

Suddenly a great tidal wave rises up in the sea. All your life you have enjoyed this beautiful blue sea, but now it rises like a monster. The volcano has stirred up the water. The tidal wave rushes into the smashed city and soon the broken stones of buildings are swirling in the wild waves. Many more hundreds who survived the volcano blast are swept into the sea and drowned. You, your sister, and most of your neighbors are lost as well.

Looters arrive to pick among the ruins after the tidal wave is gone. There is not much left to steal, but they find a few things. One of them finds a vase you painted. Although disaster has claimed your life, in some small way you live on.

■ ***Turn to page 69.***

You take a ship north to Mycenae. You are amazed at the fortress city. You climb higher and higher on craggy stones to get to the top. When you arrive atop the mighty fortress hill, you gaze out at the sea and at hills dotted with olive trees and grape vines. It's the most thrilling view you have ever seen.

You join your friend in a great hall. You drink from large golden cups or beakers and listen to minstrels talk about past adventures. You notice that the people here are not as refined as your friends in Minos. But of course you don't say that. A guest does not insult a host.

"Look at these bronze daggers," your friend says as you walk into a small room. "Do you see the gold and silver inlays on the handles? We like to put pictures of sea creatures and lions on the handles."

After you spend a week with your friend in Mycenae, you take another sea voyage to a nearby island. It is the island of Thera. It is opposite Crete.

Here are many islands, lying green and lovely in the shining sea. All the islands are in the Aegean Sea. This is where you will spend the last days of your trip. After this you must seriously work as an artist in Minos.

Thera has rich frescoes on the walls of buildings just like in Minos. You feel very much at home.

You are admiring a garden when the earth seems to rumble. Your friend turns pale. "Volcano!" he gasps.

You begin to run, but it's a small island. The volcanic mountain towers over you. An inferno of flames and exploding cinders are spewing from the top of the mountain. A great column of dark smoke fills the sky, forming clouds of ash.

You sink into the hot ash and are soon buried beneath tons of molten lava. You do not suffer much, for the intense heat kills you quickly.

■ ***Turn to page 69.***

You remain at home working on new vases. You stroll in the hills often so you can find themes in nature. If you see a very pretty wildflower, you take it home and put the design on a vase. Everybody says your designs are so lovely because you paint directly from nature.

One day you and your whole family are walking in the hills looking for wildflowers. Suddenly the earth shakes. You fall into the meadow grass in terror.

On the nearby island of Thera there has been a volcanic eruption. Great clouds of black smoke and fiery cinders rise high in the sky. When you lift your heads, you see that the blast of the eruption has shattered the buildings on Crete, too!

"How lucky that we were not at home," your mother says.

Most of the buildings have caved in on your friends and neighbors. Now a steady downpour of volcanic ash streams from the dark sky. It looks like the end of the world.

"Look!" cries your younger sister. She clings to you and hides her face. A great tidal wave washes over Crete. You are on high ground, so the destructive wave does not reach you. It sweeps over the shattered buildings and then returns to sea. You see many stones and bodies swirling in the sea.

It's the most horrible sight you have ever seen!

You never return to your house. There is nothing to return for. You move to northern Greece and pick up the pieces of your life slowly. For weeks you speak of nothing but the disaster and how lucky you were to survive it.

For a while you try to paint vases again, but there is little demand for pretty vases in this new city. Soon you marry and move to a rugged mountain village where you and your spouse become farmers. Pirates frequently attack the cities, and there is little time for vases and jewelry. You fondly remember when you were a distant relative to the royal family of Crete. With a sigh you herd your goats down a brushy path. You are living in a dark age of Greece.

■ ***Turn to page 69.***

The Lost Civilization of Atlantis

Legend has it that there once existed a beautiful island called Atlantis. It was filled with happy, peaceful people. The story comes from writings of Plato, who lived around 400 B.C. For many years people thought the legend of Atlantis was just a pretty story about an island that was destroyed by waters rising up from the sea. Some now think that Plato was writing about Crete. Around 1470 B.C. the 4900-foot volcanic mountain on the nearby island of Thera erupted violently. A 100-foot-thick layer of ash covered the surrounding lands. Under this ash archaeologists discovered the Cretan civilization.

Matching

______	1. The volcanic island near Crete	a) volcano
______	2. The natural disaster that may have destroyed Crete	b) palace
		c) Minos
______	3. A city in Crete	d) Atlantis
______	4. Plato's name for the lost civilization	e) Thera
______	5. The great Cretan building located at Knossos	

Group Activities

1. Discuss life in Crete. What were the most interesting or surprising things about living there?
2. Volcanoes and earthquakes are often located in what is called the Ring of Fire or Circle of Fire. This ring extends from the tip of South America to Alaska. Look at a world map and find out what countries are included in the Ring of Fire.
3. On a large world map, find Crete, the island of Thera, and Mycenae.

Individual Activities

1. Finish the story begun by this sentence: "I looked up and the top of the mountain blew off. I . . ."
2. Find pictures of Minoan or Cretan art and describe them in one or two paragraphs.
3. What modern sport compares to bull-leaping? Write one paragraph explaining why you would or would not have liked bull-leaping.

The Great Pharaoh and the Slaves—1235 B.C.

It is a busy time in Egypt under Ramses II. He is the Pharaoh, the king of Egypt. He has built many great buildings. He even puts his name on buildings he did not build. He wants to be remembered as a great builder. Your father plans and constructs some of the huge temples by command of the Pharaoh. You often go down to watch the buildings go up. It is very exciting. You have seen very large granaries and temples built.

Today you stand in the shade and watch. "Who are those workers who lift the heavy bricks and drag them across the sand?" you ask your father.

"Those are Israelites," your father says.

"Are they very good at such work? Is that why the Pharaoh sent them to us?" you ask.

"They used to be shepherds," says your father. "They know how to herd sheep. Now we must tell them how to do this work. The overseers keep a close watch on them."

"But why aren't they still herding their sheep?" you ask. It seems that sheepherding is a lot easier than dragging bricks around in the hot sun!

Your father laughs. "So many questions you ask, young one," he says. "Go and eat a pomegranate. Enjoy its red pulp and many seeds. Let me do my work!"

You sit under the shade of a palm tree—though it does not give much shade—and eat some figs. But you are still very curious about why the Israelites are doing such hard work.

You linger for a little while after your father goes elsewhere. One of the Israelite workers, who is about your age, stops for a drink of water from a jug. His back is shiny with sweat. You wonder if you might ask him if he likes this work better than sheepherding. Your father probably wouldn't want you to talk to the Israelites, but you are very curious.

■ ***If you talk to the Israelite, turn to page 73.***

■ ***If not, turn to page 74.***

Find out what your fate is!

You walk up to the Israelite and ask, "Where do you live?"

"Over there in those tents. The tents were put there for us while we build this granary," says the Israelite.

"Where did you live before?" you ask.

"Oh, we lived in the land of Goshen. We had fine grazing lands for our sheep."

"It's nice here, too, isn't it?" you ask. "We have a fine city. We have pools that are full of fish. Have you seen the lagoons? I go there sometimes to see the birds. There are such marvelous birds in the lagoon."

The dark-eyed Israelite nods. "Yes, it's pretty here. The meadows are covered with soft green grass. How our sheep would like to graze here! But we are slaves in Egypt. The fruit here is sweeter than honey, but it does not taste as sweet to a slave. When you cannot come and go as you want, nothing seems very nice."

You feel a bit sad at hearing that. Still, the Pharaoh is great and good. He must have excellent reasons for making slaves of these strangers. "Well, you have plenty to eat at least," you say.

"Oh yes. We have fish and meat. We have cucumbers and melons, and apples, olives, and figs. But we long to be free again," says the Israelite.

You go home to your fine house, but you keep thinking of the slave. You tell your mother about the meeting you had with the Israelite. Your mother smiles and says, "Oh, the Israelites have been here in Egypt for a long time. They complain, but the work must be done."

You have seen the great pyramids. You wonder if the Israelites built them, too.

The next week you are going with your older brother to visit a magnificent temple. It is newly built. You know that Israelite slaves built it. It makes you sad to think of all those slaves working so hard. Your brother tells you that while the temple was being built, seven Israelites were crushed by a large boulder.

You really don't want to see the temple after you hear that. You are practicing to be a scribe, so maybe you should stay home and study instead.

■ ***If you go to the temple, turn to page 75.***

■ ***If you stay home, turn to page 76.***

It would probably just upset you to talk to the Israelite, so you go home.

At your handsome house your mother is busy curling her long, lovely hair. She will go to a banquet this evening and she must look very nice. She will make her eyes beautiful with green color around them and she will wear metal bracelets. Why, she looks like a queen!

Your mother peers into her copper mirror and then smiles at you. You decide to ask her about the Israelites. "Why," she says, "they are slaves. We brought them here to work on our buildings. It is necessary, even if some of them complain. But let us talk of nicer things. We will be hunting tomorrow. Your father hopes to kill a lion or a hippopotamus and then we shall feast in the meadow."

The next day several families are off to the hunt. The families are all wealthy. You are lucky to belong to such a family because you love the excitement of the hunts. It is great fun to gather in a meadow and eat roasted pheasant and juicy, fresh fruit.

At dawn the hunters are bringing down falcons with boomerangs. The larger animals, like the elephants, are hunted with sharp spears.

You lie on the soft meadow grass and enjoy two sweet figs. You think about what you will do when you are grown. You will be a scribe and enjoy a wonderful life, you think. You have always been happy in Egypt.

Suddenly you hear a sharp noise in the papyrus thicket. You run to investigate these grasslike marsh plants. The papyrus thicket runs right along the meadow.

You see an Israelite slave sprinting along. His eyes look wild. You can see the marks of whiplashes on his back! He has been punished by the overseer for something. Now he is escaping. Perhaps he wants to go back to the land of Goshen where some of the Israelites are from.

It is your duty to tell someone that a slave is getting away. After all, the slaves belong to the Pharaoh. But in your heart you feel sorry for the slave.

■ ***If you tell someone, turn to page 77.***

■ ***If not, turn to page 78.***

You go with your brother to the temple and try to forget that slaves built it. What a marvelous place it is! Four huge seated statues of the Pharaoh, each about seventy feet high, are carved in front of the temple. The faces of the statues are so big that if you climbed up there the face would be as tall as your whole body!

"Do you see what a wonderful thing it is to build like Father does?" asks your brother. "That is why I shall be an architect like him when I am grown."

"It is very noble to be a scribe, too," you point out. "To be a good scribe I will have to memorize many symbols. As many as seven hundred."

Your brother smiles. You hate it when he smiles like that. It makes you feel small and silly. "Yes," he says. "It is true that a scribe is held in honor in Egypt. But I cannot see myself sitting cross-legged on the floor all my life waiting for somebody to dictate to me."

"But what of the future?" you ask. "I will be writing papyrus scrolls, telling the great stories of Egypt. How will people know how great we are if I do not write about it? Hundreds of years from now people will know of us and how we lived because of scribes like me."

"Oh, but I would rather have people look at the great buildings I have built," says your brother. "Any person who sees this temple will know that great people built it. What are a few words on paper made from papyrus grass compared to that?"

You look up at the temple. Truly great minds planned the temple. You do not doubt that. Your father is a great man. He and the other architects of Egypt have great and noble ideas. But who will write about the labor that built the temple? That must be remembered too.

You smile at your brother. "I think we will both make our marks on history. You will make yours in your way. I will make mine in my way."

■ ***Turn to page 79.***

You study the symbols of your language as your mother makes the midday meal of roasted chicken.

Soon an old man appears at your door. He is a storyteller. His head is full of wonderful stories. But, like most people in Egypt, he cannot read or write. That is why you study so hard to be a scribe. You think it is wonderful to be able to write on the papyrus scrolls.

"Child," says the old man. "Have you heard the tale of the puffed-up man and the elephant?"

How he loves to share his tales. They are interesting, and they also teach virtue.

"Tell me, wise man," you say respectfully.

The old man sits down and begins his tale: "Once there was a puffed-up young man who went hunting elephants. When he met up with important men he never cast down his face as he should have. He always looked at them boldly. As he went to hunt the elephant, he took his servant along. The servant said, 'I will see that we are not trampled by elephants, for I have been on many elephant hunts, and this is your first.'

"Well, the puffed-up man laughed and said, 'Fool, there is nothing any man knows better than I. I shall lead the way on the elephant hunt. No harm shall befall me.' So the puffed-up young man rushed right into the path the elephants used on their way to get water and he was trampled to death.

"The servant carried the man's broken body home. The tearful family asked, 'Was he trampled by elephants?' 'No,' said the servant. 'He was trampled by pride.'"

You remember this tale, and when you become a scribe you write it down. You write down the wisdom of many who cannot write for themselves. You have saved the old man's tale for all time.

You are proud to be a scribe because you know that hundreds of years from now your words will tell people about Egypt. They will look at Egypt's great buildings and be impressed. But people like you will write the ideas that were in the hearts and souls of the Egyptian people.

■ ***Turn to page 79.***

"Look," you shout, "there goes a runaway slave!"

The men in the hunting party take chase. They grab the Israelite and drag him back. When you see him up close, you notice he is about your age. You feel a little more sorry when you see that.

"I could not bear dragging the heavy stones anymore," says the Israelite. "I am a shepherd's son. I am not a stoneworker."

The Israelite is flogged very cruelly. You are now truly sorry that you shouted. You wouldn't want to drag heavy stones in the heat, either!

The slave is taken away and your father and the other men continue their hunting. Soon they bring back a dead elephant. They are in very high spirits over their good luck.

Soon you are feasting and talking about the hunt. All the brave hunters tell in detail about the narrow escapes they had. To hear them talk you think that each one came within a hair of being killed, including your father. It is so exciting to hear the stories.

You feel very lucky to be a young Egyptian.

As you grow older, you hear disturbing stories about the Israelites. There are leaders among them who promise to lead their people out of Egyptian slavery. You hear a lot of grumbling about how troublesome the Israelites are. But you remember the poor slave who tried to escape that day and was flogged.

When the Israelites finally do escape from Egypt, they will make a feast to celebrate it—Passover. And forever after they will eat *matzo*, unleavened bread, and read the story of their escape to remember how precious freedom is.

But as for you, you become a scribe and you are not troubled very much by slaves. After all, there have always been slaves in Egypt. It just seems the natural way of things, though you are glad you are not a slave yourself.

■ ***Turn to page 79.***

You say nothing as the Israelite vanishes into the wilderness. Then, a little while later, as you wander in the papyrus thicket quite a distance away, you see the boy again. You see that he is very young, about your age. You have a loaf of bread and some figs with you, and you hold them towards him.

"Are you hungry?" you ask. "I have already eaten too much. My stomach hurts. You can have these."

The boy eagerly takes the bread and figs. He acts as if he has not eaten in a long time.

"Were you once a sheepherder?" you ask him.

"Many of us are shepherds or fishers," he says.

"Is it very hard to work on making bricks and building the great granaries and temples?" you ask.

"We have bread enough, but it is a hard life. The overseers have rods. They say 'Be not idle' and if we stop a moment, or work slower, we are struck."

"Where will you go now?" you ask.

"I will hide until all the Israelites escape from Egypt. We will flee into the desert and be free again. God will lead us out of slavery," says the Israelite.

You watch the boy hurry away. You know in your heart that what you did was not quite right. All the slaves belong to the Pharaoh. You kept silent while one of the Pharaoh's slaves got away.

You could not do otherwise, though. And now you hurry back to the meadow where the men are returning with an elephant that has been killed. There are shouts and laughter and stories to be told. Every hunter will tell how he was almost killed by the elephants. Your father will tell the best story. He always does.

When you are a scribe you will write of your father's adventures and what it is like to be an Egyptian. You may even write about the Israelite.

■ ***Turn to page 79.***

Wonders of Egypt

The Great Pyramid of Cheops in Egypt is a truly amazing building. It was built around 2700 B.C. It is as high as a 42-story modern building. It covers 13 acres. There are 6 million tons of stone in it. That's enough stone to build a 10-foot wall all around the country of France.

The Egyptians did not have modern engineering tools. They just had ropes and levers. They would build a mud ramp to drag the stones to the top. Thousands of masons and slaves worked for 20 years to build the Great Pyramid. Today, almost 5,000 years later, the marvelous building still stands.

Matching

______	1. Around 1235 B.C. he ruled Egypt	a) Pharaoh
______	2. The king of Egypt was called	b) pomegranate
______	3. Some of the slaves in Egypt were	c) Ramses II
______	4. The Great Pyramid was named for	d) Israelites
______	5. Fruit with red pulp and many seeds	e) Cheops

Group Activities

1. Discuss what life is like in Egypt today. Find out who rules, what kind of government they have, and how the average person lives. What is the average income? Are most children educated? What is the life span?
2. The Egyptian writing system was called *hieroglyphics*. Make a poster with ten common words or expressions in hieroglyphics.
3. Do you think slavery in Egypt was easier or harder for the slaves than it was in the United States in the eighteenth and nineteenth centuries?

Individual Activities

1. If you had lived in Egypt, would you have preferred being a builder or a scribe? Explain your answer in one paragraph.
2. Find pictures of the pyramids and make models from clay or cardboard.
3. Imagine you are an Israelite slave in Egypt. Describe your feelings in one or two paragraphs.

A Gift in the Land of Canaan—950 B.C.

You are a young Hebrew in the land of Canaan.[1] King Solomon rules your land. You have never met him and you don't expect to. But you respect him as the king. Your land is green with rich orchards and rolling hills. The fig trees are your favorite. There is nothing more delicious than a sweet, juicy fig!

One of the nice things about living here is that there are bright colors everywhere. Your father wears bright red and blue coats. Your mother usually wears bright green. You can see all the colors of the rainbow here. Pomegranates and saffron give yellow dye. The madder root and safflower give red colors. The woad plant gives blue, and from snails you can get a bright purple dye.

You want to give your mother a special gift. You are trying to decide what it will be. She likes perfume a lot. Nobody smells as nice as your mother! She puts perfume on her hair and her bed.

"Oh, doesn't cinnamon have a lovely smell?" your mother has said. "It comes all the way from India. And the perfumes from flowers are wonderful, too."

You probably should give your mother perfume. But she likes ointment, too. You might get her an ivory bowl to mix spices and oils. She rubs olive oil and spices into her skin to protect it against the hot, windy weather.

You have only a few coins as you set out to buy the gift. You hope you have enough for something that is truly nice.

At the marketplace you see a stall filled with tiny burnt-clay jars for keeping perfumes. Across the path is another stall with bowls made of limestone, ivory, and alabaster. They have little pestles, or hammers, for crushing spices into powder to put into oil for ointments.

■ ***If you go to the perfume stall, turn to page 83.***

■ ***If you go to the ointment stall, turn to page 84.***

Find out what your fate is!

---

[1] Palestine

You go to the perfume stall. How good it smells here! There are dainty perfume flasks and sweet-smelling aloes and myrrh.

"Yes? What do you want?" asks the merchant.

Just as you are about to decide, a voice comes from afar. It is like a wail. "Have pity! I am a poor blind beggar! I need bread."

You see an old man in rags on the road. He looks very thin and hungry. It must be terrible, you think, to be blind and not able to see the beautiful world. But it must be even worse to be blind and poor. Your parents have taught you to show kindness to the poor. According to the prophets, your teachers, showing kindness is right and just.

But if you give away any of your coins, you will not have enough left for the fine gift you want. You have long dreamed of your mother's face lighting up with joy to receive a gift from you.

Maybe someone else will help the blind beggar. You watch hopefully as a well-dressed man hurries by. Surely he will stop and listen to the beggar's cries. But he does not. Nor do two merchants who rush by just as fast.

"Well," says the perfume merchant in an impatient voice, "do you want to buy something or not?"

"Just a moment," you say. You see a young man coming. He looks well fed and content. Surely he will be so thankful for his own good fortune that he will toss a few coins at the beggar!

The beggar calls out for help when he hears the young man's footsteps, but no coins are tossed his way.

Now it's up to you. Do you share the few coins you have with the beggar? Or do you buy the perfume and hurry home, hoping someone else will eventually help the beggar?

■ ***If you buy the perfume, turn to page 85.***

■ ***If you share your coins, turn to page 86.***

You hurry to the ointment stall. There are large jugs filled with spices. There are olive oil jars, too.

"Mastic! Mastic!" a girl about your age shouts.

You turn sharply to see a man selling mastic. These yellowish-white balls are taken from the pistachio bush and make a wonderful chewing gum. It is good for your teeth and gums, too. You love it!

"Just a little mastic, please," you say. You take the mastic and put it in your mouth. As you chew you continue to look at ointment. You decide on an ivory bowl. But then you realize you don't have enough coins. You are just a bit short, because of the mastic you bought.

"Well," suggests the merchant, "why not give your mother a nice mirror? I have some here that you could buy at a lesser price than the ivory bowl."

You look at the brightly polished metal discs. Your mother already has a mirror. Why would she want another one? She does not look at herself all the time. She is much too busy for that.

"What about curling pins for her hair?" asks the merchant. "Most women can use them."

"Maybe," you say, but curling pins do not sound like the fine gift you had in mind! Why did you have to weaken and buy the mastic?

"What about henna?" asks the merchant. "Your mother can take the henna powder and make her hair red. Or she might make her fingernails red."

You have never seen your mother use henna to make *anything* red! She is very pretty with her nice dark-brown hair. But you suppose you would not displease her if you brought her curling pins or a mirror. And that is all you can afford.

■ ***If you buy the mirror, turn to page 87.***

■ ***If you buy the curling pins, turn to page 88.***

You must have the delightful little perfume flask for your mother. You try not to look at the poor man as you buy the perfume.

You run home with the perfume. Your mother is in the house making the evening meal. She is roasting lamb and making bread.

"Mother," you say. "I have a gift for you."

Your mother comes and takes the perfume. A big smile comes to her face. "Oh, this is so lovely. This is my favorite perfume! (You aren't sure that's true. Your mother would say that just to make you feel good. But it *is* a nice fragrance.)

You are so happy to see your mother touching the perfume to her hair.

"I wanted to give you something you would like," you say. "I almost shared my coins with a beggar at the marketplace, but then I couldn't have bought the nice perfume."

Suddenly your mother looks sad. "You gave nothing to a beggar?"

"No, I didn't. I was afraid I wouldn't have enough left for good perfume. I so wanted to make you happy."

But your mother begins to softly weep. You rush to her side. "Oh, do you not like the perfume after all?" you ask.

"I do like the perfume," your mother says. "But kindness is sweeter than any perfume. I would rather you had shared with the beggar and bought me a less costly gift. Even if you had given me nothing and instead helped the poor man, I would be happier."

You feel very sad. But your mother is right. The poor beggar may still be there, crying for bread that never comes.

■ ***Turn to page 89.***

"Here," you say. "Take these coins. It will help a little." You have given the man half your coins.

"Many thanks," he says, stumbling off at once to buy bread.

Now you return to the perfume stall to buy your mother's gift. But you don't have enough money left to buy the gift you wanted.

"Away with you," says the perfume merchant. "What you have there is not enough to bother with. Others with money want to buy. You are taking up space before my stall."

You feel terrible as you start for home with no gift for your mother. She works hard, and she deserves a nice gift.

Suddenly you see something bright yellow in a field. It's a loosestrife bush. The leaves of this shrub are used to make henna, a red dye. But the flowers are delicate yellow sprays. You have seen women wearing these yellow flowers in their hair. Your mother's nice thick brown hair would look very good with a spray of loosestrife flowers in it.

You pick several sprays and hurry towards home.

"Mother," you say, "I was going to buy you some fine perfume but a poor beggar was crying for bread. I shared my coins with him. And then I didn't have enough left to buy the perfume. So I have nothing for you but some flowers for your hair."

Your mother's eyes sparkle with tears. Oh! She is disappointed. But no, wait—she is smiling!

"Dear child," she says, "how proud I am of you this moment. You have a kind heart. Not all the perfumes of Arabia could make me as happy as I am now."

Your mother puts the yellow flowers in her hair. How beautiful she looks. How happy you are!

■ ***Turn to page 89.***

You decide to buy the mirror. Your mother will be able to use that. It's not as nice a gift as you had hoped to buy, but it will have to do.

"What have you there?" asks a boy about your age.

"A mirror. I'm giving it to my mother."

"She probably already has a mirror," says the boy. "I have a nice burnt-clay jar I will trade you for the mirror."

You look at the jar. "It is very nice. Mother could keep perfume in it. I'll make the trade."

As you walk towards home you meet an old man. "What do you carry there?" he asks.

"A burnt-clay jar for my mother. I plan to give it to her as a gift," you say.

"Ah, I know your good mother," says the old man. "I think she would like a small jar of honey much more. I will trade it for the burnt-clay jar."

You know that your mother does like honey on her bread. You make the trade and then hurry on. When you are almost home, you meet a neighbor woman. She sees the honey you are carrying. "Are you taking that honey to your mother?" she asks.

"Yes, I want to give my mother a gift."

"A gift should be something that lasts," says the woman. "The honey will soon be gone and then she will not remember the gift. I will take the honey from you and give you something your mother will like much more."

You know this woman is familiar with your mother. She would know what kind of gift would please your mother. So you say, "Very well. I will make the trade."

The woman takes the honey and gives you a polished metal disc. "Your mother can always use another mirror," says the woman.

You smile and take the mirror. You run the rest of the way home and give your mother the mirror. She seems to like it very much. She seems to be pleased that you thought enough to buy her *any* gift.

■ ***Turn to page 89.***

You buy the curling pins and hurry toward home. You stop when you see an old man shouting at a crowd of people.

"Who is the fellow with the long white beard?" you ask a man in the crowd.

"He is a prophet," says the man. "He says we are all wicked people because we think too much about wearing fine clothing and looking nice."

You listen for a few minutes.

"Curling your hair and wearing beards are signs of false pride," the prophet shouts. "Soon we will all be bald!"

You shudder. Maybe what the old prophet is saying is true. Maybe everybody in the land of Canaan is too interested in looking nice. And you bought curling pins for your mother!

You see a stall where a man is selling fruit. You hurry over and say, "Could I trade these curling pins for some nice, sweet fruit?"

The man offers you a basket of figs that look very good indeed. You make the trade.

How good the figs look! But maybe they don't taste as good as they look. You sit under an olive tree and try one of the figs. Oh, it is delicious and juicy. But are all of them this good? Perhaps you should try one more.

Just then you hear a stern voice. "Why do you sit under the tree stuffing yourself with figs?" It is the voice of the white-haired prophet.

"These are a gift for my mother," you say. "But I am making sure they are good enough for her."

"You have eaten almost all of them," scolds the prophet. "Hasten home before you make a complete glutton of yourself!"

You almost tell the prophet that it is his fault you have figs instead of curling pins for your mother. But you decide not to argue with a stern prophet. You hurry home and give your mother the figs that are left. She seems pleased with your gift.

■ ***Turn to page 89.***

King Solomon

King Solomon ruled from about 960 to 925 B.C. The name *Solomon* means "peaceful" in Hebrew. Solomon ruled a powerful empire and he built many great buildings. His temple at Jerusalem, Yahweh Temple, was the most famous. This temple was built with cedar, fir, and pine trees. It was overlaid with pure gold. The floor was made of marble. Even the nails used to hammer the wood together were made of gold. Great golden angels stood in the temple. When the temple was done, Solomon and his people began to pray.

Matching

______	1. The land of Canaan was	a) Solomon
______	2. Cinnamon was brought all the way from	b) India
______	3. This man's name meant "peaceful" in Hebrew	c) temple
______	4. Spices were mixed in bowls made of	d) Palestine
______	5. Solomon's greatest building in Jerusalem was a	e) ivory

Group Activities

1. King Solomon was considered a wise man. Discuss these sayings attributed to him.

   A soft answer turns away wrath.
   Pride goes before destruction.
   Wisdom is better than riches.
   A merry heart is good medicine.
   Let another praise you, not your own mouth.

2. On a map of the ancient world find the empire of Israel. It stretched north to Hamath, west to Joppa and Gaza, and south to the Red Sea. How does this compare to the modern state of Israel?
3. Make a mural of the flowers mentioned in the selection. Draw pictures of loosestrife, madder, safflower, and woad.

Individual Activities

1. Write one paragraph about the gift you ended up choosing and why you chose it.
2. Find out where the prized purple dye of these ancient times came from. Write a paragraph about it.
3. Write a paragraph about one of the following:
   a) Queen of Sheba
   b) King Hiram

An Athenian Dream—500 B.C.

You are a young Athenian interested in drama and sports. You think Athens is a fine place to live. Most of the other people who live here agree.

Your cube-shaped mud-brick house is brightly [illegible] on the inside. It's very comfortable and [illegible]inted vases in your house show scenes of ships and famous battles as well as peaceful scenes of everyday life.

You enjoy going to the great open-air theaters to see comedies and tragedies. You would like to become an actor in one of these plays during a drama festival. You are very good at storytelling, and everybody says you have gifts that would make you a fine performer. For one thing, you have a nice, loud voice. When you are telling a story you sound very dramatic and everybody listens closely.

But sports is another pleasure in your life. You have long admired the athletes who perform in the Olympic games. The Olympic games attract athletes from all over Greece. You especially enjoy watching the runners, because you like to run. You have often wondered if you could become a champion at the Olympic games. The winners receive a garland of olive leaves, but that's not the important part of winning. The important part is that when you win you know that you are the very best.

It would be truly wonderful to be the best runner, discus thrower, or wrestler. The cheers of the crowd would sound very sweet to your ears, but in your heart would be the highest reward: knowing you are the best.

■ *If you work to improve your dramatic skills, turn to page 93.*

■ *If you train for the Olympics, turn to page 94.*

Find out what your fate is!

You prepare to take part in a dramatic play. It's a tragedy, a sad play. Many Greek plays are about great people with high ideals who must suffer a lot. The audiences like such plays because it shows that even important people have to suffer misfortunes like ordinary people.

You will not act in the play, but you will be a part of it. You will stand between the actors and the spectators as part of the chorus. You and the other members of the chorus will speak, dance, and sing. You will make comments about the actions in the play.

When the big day arrives, you are very excited. The theater is like a bowl. Thousands of stone seats are built up into a hill in a semicircle. The stage is down at the bottom. This design helps the actors to be heard far from the stage. It amazes you that the people sitting high up in the theater can hear the actors' voices.

You want to perform your small part well. Then maybe someday you will have a real acting part.

The actors wear bronze masks to show their emotions. They will be so far from many in the audience that it's hard to see a smile or a frown. But if the mask shows an angry face, the audience will know the character is angry. The masks are bright and clearly expressive.

You speak your small line very well. You sing well, too. Older members of the play praise you.

"You are very good," says an older actor. "You should train more and act in a play yourself."

You are excited by the idea. You could be one of the actors wearing the beautiful bronze masks!

But your sister says, "You enjoy acting because you like to perform in front of people. You play the lyre very well. Why don't you become a musician? It is much easier to be a musician than an actor. You will have the same pleasure of performing in front of people."

It is true that you enjoy playing the lyre, and even the flute.

■ ***If you become a musician, turn to page 95.***

■ ***If you become an actor, turn to page 96.***

You decide to train for the Olympics. You must train your body to be its best. You eat wheat and barley porridge and plenty of cheese and vegetables. You like fish better than mutton and pork. It seems to give you more energy. You love fresh fruit, too. It makes you feel good inside.

You get plenty of rest and try to harden your body against discomfort. On cold days your room is often heated with a coal-filled stove. Now you leave the stove unlighted. You sleep in a cold room.

You try to run up hills that are steeper and steeper. At first you are so out of breath you must rest often. Your chest hurts and you fear you are dying. But little by little it becomes easier. You can sprint for long distances and not be tired. The longer you run, the stronger you become. And you have a strange sort of joy when you run. Sometimes it feels as if you are flying.

You train under a special coach who tells you how to strengthen your leg muscles. You learn how to move your legs before you run so you don't get leg cramps.

At last the day of the Olympic games is here. How thrilled you are to be a part of this great event. You set off for the stadium early in the morning.

"What a wonderful thing these games are," says a fellow competitor. "They are open to everybody."

"Yes," you agree. "You don't have to be from a wealthy family to compete. Why, it was a simple cook, Coroebus, who won the first Olympic prize."

You take the oath that all the athletes take. You promise to follow the rules of the game and not cheat. You cannot imagine how anyone would cheat!

The torch is carried from the temple to the games. Now, finally, you begin to run. Faster and faster you go. This is the race of your life.

You win the race and receive the wreath of olive leaves. Oh, how marvelous you feel at this moment!

Suddenly you are grabbed by an excited man. "Since you are the fastest runner, would you carry an important message to Athens? Our glorious army has defeated the Persians at Marathon!"

You would be proud to carry such a message. But it would mean running almost thirty miles, and you are exhausted from your run today.

■ ***If you run to Athens, turn to page 97.***

■ ***If you don't, turn to page 98.***

You decide you would rather become a musician. So you practice your lyre. It's a stringed instrument like the harp. Your lyre is made out of tortoiseshell. As you get better, you will play the cithara, which is a larger, heavier harp.

You also have a nice singing voice. You plan to sing poetry for noble families who will hire you.

After much practice, you go to a dinner party to entertain some people. You are trembling with excitement. If you do well here, you will be invited to other places.

You recite and sing poetry about love and hate, joy and sadness. Soon people are smiling and cheering. They eat and drink, and seem to enjoy you more as time goes by. You are less nervous, too. You are playing beautifully and singing well.

Now you try to recite some of your own poetry. It isn't as good as the old poetry, but it's quite nice. The people at the party seem to like it.

After the dinner party, everybody is talking about the exciting young musician who came to entertain.

"My brother is having guests over," says one of the wealthy men. "You must come to his party and perform!"

A woman approaches you and urges you to come to her friend's party as well.

You are on your way!

Sometimes you recite the long poems of Hesiod, a poet who wrote *Works and Days*. The poem urges such virtues as justice, thrift, industry, neighborliness, and good citizenship. Your Athenian audiences really appreciate that. But the most popular works you read are Homer's *Iliad* and *Odyssey*. The dramatic tale of the siege of Troy keeps your audiences enchanted. In a way it is like being an actor, only better. You can recite, sing, and play your lyre and cithara.

Your life is full of joy and music.

■ ***Turn to page 99.***

You decide to practice to be an actor. You work under the guidance of an older actor who advises you on the use of your voice and gestures.

"Dramatic gestures are very important," he says, "for even when you wear the angry mask to show rage, you must also make wide, sweeping gestures to show your emotion. This makes what is happening clear to the audience. You cannot regard the mask as taking away your obligation to show emotion with your entire body."

"Shall I try to act in comedies or tragedies?" you ask.

"Comedy is a lower form of the play," your teacher tells you. He then says, "Try to perform in plays that surprise. The best play is one that surprises. I do not like it when everybody expects the end."

You work on your voice and gestures. Finally the day arrives for you to act in your first play. You will be in a play by Aeschylus. There are two actors in this play. Everything will depend on you and the other actor.

You are very nervous just before the play. The other actor leans over and whispers, "It is normal to be nervous. Even I am nervous and I have been in many plays. If you are not nervous, then you don't care if you are good or not."

When you begin to speak, you look out at all the people. These are hundreds of them. Your voice comes out too softly.

"Louder!" mutters the other actor.

You try to raise your voice, but it comes out as a large squeak. It was one thing being in the chorus with many others. Now everybody is looking at you alone. Oh, this is terrible! Your voice feels as if it is frozen. You want to run from the stage and hide somewhere!

You somehow get through the performance, but you know you did badly. You never want to be in another play. You made a mistake to choose this profession!

You quickly decide to be a teacher instead of an actor.

■ ***Turn to page 99.***

You are so full of pride in your victory that you feel it is your duty to run to Athens. You must carry the word of the glorious victory at Marathon.

You sprint from the stadium to the cheers of the audience. You are able to do anything. You are sure of it.

Across the meadows you race. Your feet trample a crocus here and there. You run past willows and poplars. They are just a blur to you as you go. As you run up a hill you see bare, rocky slopes and pines. Higher and higher you go, through stands of oak, chestnut, and beech.

Your chest has begun to ache. Your heart feels like a hot coal within you. But you must press on. You think of the battle of Marathon and what other young Greeks went through to achieve the victory. This gives you renewed courage.

Darius, the Persian, has tried to crush Greece. He calls himself the Great King. But in your mind people who are not Athenians are almost barbarians. Your own civilization is the best of all; you are sure of it. What would have become of the Greek civilization if Darius had won? You shudder to think of it!

On you go to bring news of victory to the waiting city. You will tell how the Athenians drove the Persians into the sea. What joy and pride will fill your beloved city of Athens.

You are gasping for breath. How can you run any farther? Your legs do not seem to be connected to your body. Your breath comes in short, painful gasps.

You run on, though, over the olive-green meadows. There, before you, lies Athens. You are almost there. The temples with their reddish-brown terra cotta tiles and blue walls sparkle in the sun. You must go only a few more yards . . .

You stumble and fall. Your arms fly out. You lie still upon the grass, face down. Your brave heart has given out. You could not quite reach Athens.

■ ***Turn to page 99.***

You don't think you could run to Athens. Another, more experienced, Olympian is given the honor.

You travel home to tell your mother of your triumph at the Olympics. Women are not allowed at the Olympics now, but later this will change.

Just ten years after the victory of the Athenians at Marathon, the Persians threaten to invade again. The new Persian king is Xerxes. He attacks and captures Athens!

You must fight to regain your beloved Athens.

You are in the Battle of Salamis. The Persian fleet is lured into the narrow strait between the island of Salamis and the mainland of Greece. The fierce battle begins.

Xerxes' fighters wear helmets and carry shields. They carry javelins, which are light spears. The prow of the Persian ship rams your ship. Soon the Persians leap aboard your ship. You fight them spear to spear. It's a terrible massacre on both sides. Your spear goes into the heart of a Persian. He dies at your feet.

The Phoenicians are fighting alongside the Persians. They are even better than the Persians at sea battles. But you hold your own. Even with a javelin wound in your thigh, you fight on. You don't know how many of the enemy you have killed, but your shield is stained with much blood.

At last you fall with another wound. You are carried to safety. Your wounds heal and the Greeks win the Battle of Salamis. The Persians are driven off.

Your young life has been filled with Olympian glory and success in a terrible sea battle. But now you must return to the real world. You must make a living for the rest of your life.

You learn from your father how to produce olive oil. You marry and begin to raise olive trees and extract oil from the fruit.

■ ***Turn to page 99.***

Who Was Homer?

The *Iliad* and the *Odyssey* are magnificent poems which were recited in Greece about three thousand years go. Legends say that a blind man named Homer made up the poems. Many people believe that the poems were made up by many storytelling poets who wandered around. Each one added to the poems and made them a little better. Then, at last, the finished poems were written down. We know little about Homer, but we do know that these poems are among the greatest works ever produced in the world.

Matching

______	1. The athletic games of Greece	a) mud-brick
______	2. The legendary author of the *Iliad* and the *Odyssey*	b) blind
______	3. Many Athenian houses were made of	c) Homer
______	4. The Olympic winners won a	d) garland of olive leaves
______	5. Legends tell us that Homer was	e) Olympics

Group Activities

1. Read aloud parts of the *Iliad* and the *Odyssey*. Discuss the language and style.
2. Make a large poster showing the three major kinds of Greek columns: Doric, Ionic, and Corinthian.
3. Write a one-act play based on the story of Pandora, Atlas, Jason, or other figures from Greek mythology. Perform it in class.

Individual Activities

1. The following popular sayings are based on Greek mythology. Find out what each one means and write a paragraph about it.

   A Pandora's box   An Achilles heel   A Trojan horse
2. Read the story of Phidippides and the origins of the marathon. You will find the story under *Marathon* in a a good encyclopedia.
3. Read part of a Greek play such as *The Birds* or *The Frogs*. In one paragraph describe how you liked it.

A Spartan Life— 469 B.C.

You are a young Spartan facing a hard life. You were sent to a military camp at the age of seven. How you remember that first day!

"There shall be no shoes or sandals here!" shouted the overseer. "You must grow tough and hardy by going barefoot. Then you will be able to climb rocky mountains and clamber down cliffs. You will be able to spring and run and leap faster than any enemy you may have to fight."

Your feet were very sore at first. Then they grew hard and calloused. You were given one garment to wear in winter and summer. When you first arrived you said, "But surely in winter we would need some sort of heavy cloak." Just for saying that, you were whipped! You learned fast. You did not make such comments again. You must be able to endure heat and cold without a word of complaint.

Even at mealtimes you suffer. There is never enough food. You are starved on purpose. You get only a bit of stale bread and some hard cheese. The overseer says, "You must be ready to work or fight on an empty stomach. Cravings for food must be overcome."

You must, above all, be obedient. It is a terrible wrong to disobey.

Yet how you dislike this harsh life! Sometimes you envy the wild birds and beasts of the field who can run to and fro as they please.

Today the overseer gathers you all together. "You have reached the point in your training when you must learn to live by your wits. Someday you may be part of an army in another land. You will have no rations. You must then live by taking what you need from the local people. So today you will receive no food. You must set out from here and steal your food from the helots."

The helots are the serfs of Sparta. They must live and work where the citizens (free people) tell them to go. If they attempt to leave their farms they are killed.

You are sent out at night after a day of hunger. You must find the farm of a helot and rob him. But you are sick with fear. How much more of this harsh life can you endure? You are tempted to run home to your parents' house and tell them how you feel.

■ ***If you try to steal from a helot, turn to page 103.***

■ ***If you go home, turn to page 104.***

Find out what your fate is!

You cannot disobey your orders. Being a good Spartan means always to obey. So you slowly crawl down a rocky cliff. The helot in the farm below has chickens. You can easily break into the enclosure and steal three or four. You can wring their necks, pluck their feathers, and enjoy roasted chicken over an open fire in the hills.

You are shaking as you draw closer to the small farm. The moon is moving like a ship behind some clouds. This is the perfect moment to steal. Everything is dark. In another few minutes the moon will emerge from the cloudy cover and the valley will be bathed in moonlight. Then the helot householder may come out and attack you. A helot would of course be killed for murdering a free citizen, but what if he murders you and buries your body? Nobody would know what happened to you.

You hurry forward now. You try to recall all the instruction you have had. A Spartan youth is brave and quick. A Spartan youth does what he must, quickly and efficiently, and then he is gone like the wind. Soon you will reach the enclosure. But the moon has come out into an open space. It's like daylight in the valley!

With a mighty leap you land beside the enclosure. The chickens begin to squawk loudly. If the householder is a light sleeper he will be awake and at the door in seconds.

You rip the gate of the enclosure open. You try to grab a nearby hen, but she beats her wings frantically and escapes.

"Thief!" cries a gruff voice from inside the house. You have been discovered! The man sounds tough. He may have a weapon. At the very least he has arms as hard as old olive-tree trunks!

Should you make a last desperate grab for a chicken, or flee at once without confronting the helot householder?

■ ***If you try to get a chicken, turn to page 105.***

■ ***If you flee, turn to page 106.***

You strike out for home in the darkness, racing on your hard, bare feet. How you long for the life you knew at home when you were small! There was good fresh bread, and fish and vegetables. You were not always hungry and afraid as you are now.

When you reach the family home, you come face to face with your father. He has gotten up to open the door and now he stares at you. He could not look more angry if you were a thief!

"What is wrong? Why do you come here like this?" he asks sharply. Your father is already old and gray-haired. He was a soldier all his life. Like all good Spartans he gave his young years to Sparta and then settled down to marriage in his later life.

"Father, I could not bear the harsh life," you say. "Please take me in and give me something to eat." Already you feel very guilty. You are ashamed of what you have done.

Your mother now stands beside your father. Her face is hard, too. You remember when your older brother left for a battle. Your mother told him to come back carrying his shield as a victor or to come back dead, lying on his shield. Now she says, "Go back to the camp. Admit the wicked thing you have done by running away. Take the punishment they give you without a whimper."

"Unhappy child," says your father, "you will not enter this home in disgrace."

"Begone, shameful one," scolds your mother.

You turn and hurry away. How can you return to the military camp? How can you explain what you have done? You will be severely punished. You can already feel the savage sting of the whip. You have seen others whipped almost to death for much lesser offenses.

As you near the camp, you wonder what you might do to lessen the punishment. Could you perhaps say you were away so long because you were attacked by a helot? Or should you tell the awful truth?

■ ***If you lie, turn to page 107.***

■ ***If you tell the truth, turn to page 108.***

You lunge for the chickens and fall flat on your face. The angry helot is upon you, thrashing you. He dashes you in the skull with a rock. Stunned, you still manage to rise up, hitting him back. Somehow you escape before he comes after you again. The moon is behind the clouds and it's dark as you scramble up the brushy hill.

When you reach a creek, you lie down and bathe your throbbing head with cool water. The pain lessens a little. But you are still dizzy when you rise and continue your quest for food. You must find another helot to rob.

You walk half the night before you come upon another helot farm where you see animals within easy reach. But before you can approach it, you see two helots in the pens with the animals! Both are bigger than you. They have risen early to do their work, for it is almost dawn. Almost dawn and you have failed!

Just then you see an old helot coming down the path with a loaf of bread and a basket of vegetables. He is getting an early start to market.

You confront the man on the path and shout, "I will have those!" You grab the bread and the basket. The old man is frail and weak. He does not resist.

You quickly eat a hunk of bread and a tomato before hurrying back towards your camp. But a sound makes you pause. The old man is weeping!

For a second you feel pity. Perhaps that was all the old man had. But then you remember your training. To pity is to show weakness. A Spartan never shows weakness.

You return to camp and the overseer praises you for not only finding enough to eat, but getting even more than you needed. You glow with pride.

When you grow up you fight in the Peloponnesian War between Athens and Sparta. You fight ruthlessly and kill many Athenians. You become a great general. You become a hero, too. The story of how you died in battle after killing 33 Athenians will often be told to children. In 404 B.C. Athens will fall to Sparta. You will be remembered as one of Sparta's greatest generals, who gave his life for his city-state.

■ ***Turn to page 109.***

You race away and escape before the helot comes out. But you still have no food. You must find and rob another helot before dawn. You cannot return to camp a failure.

You come to another farm and see a young kid goat. You could sneak down and take it while the moon is dark. You creep down to the farm and snatch the goat, killing it swiftly with a knife.

You hurry into the brushy hills to make a fire and feast on your kill. You will bring what's left back to camp. You feel proud to have stolen a helot's goat.

As you begin to make your fire, you already feel like a grown Spartan soldier. This is how it will be when you are at war. You will be raiding the countryside and stealing from the enemy. You will be a strong, self-reliant soldier. Other men will look up to you.

You reach for a branch of a tree to break off. You need it for your fire. Suddenly the rocks beneath your feet give way. You slip! You frantically try to catch yourself on the shrub near your hand. But you uproot it and continue tumbling down the hill. Your leg is twisted before you reach the bottom.

You are in terrible pain. Somehow you manage to crawl back to camp anyway. But you are shocked at how you are greeted. The overseer looks at your leg and says, "It looks like a permanent injury. Of what use will you be to Sparta now?"

"I will surely heal and be strong again," you say hopefully. But it does not happen. You can walk with the aid of a stick, but you know you will not grow strong enough to be a soldier.

"It would have been better if you had died in the fall," says the overseer. "Sparta has no use for the sick and injured. You know that when a weak baby is born it is not tended. It is left to die."

One dark night one of your companions sends an arrow into your heart. He does not do it out of cruelty. He thinks he is being a good Spartan. If you cannot be strong and healthy, he thinks you are only a burden to Sparta.

■ ***Turn to page 109.***

When you enter camp late, you meet the overseer. "Where have you been?" he demands. "You were supposed to return at dawn and you have been gone two days."

"On my way to steal from a helot, I was attacked and injured. For a whole day I lay wounded and unable to return," you say.

"You have been trained to fight. Yet you were overcome by a wretched slave?" says the grim-faced overseer.

You look down sadly. You must show total respect for your overseer. "There is no excuse for my stupidity. I was caught by surprise. I am a fool," you say.

"You failed in your mission. What if you had been in enemy country? The soldier who can't find provisions is the soldier who starves and is of no use to Sparta," says the overseer.

"I deserve the worst of punishment," you say.

Other youths come with whips. You must stand in silence as you are cruelly whipped. You must not cry out or even groan.

At last the punishment is over. But you do not sleep for many nights because of the pain. Anger rises in your heart. But you must not direct the anger against your overseer. He was only doing his duty. It is the Spartan way. You must save the hurt and anger you feel and use it someday against the enemies of Sparta. You must use this experience to become a ruthless soldier.

You become a savage Spartan soldier when you grow up. Everyone remarks about the fury you show in battle. You win many victories in the Peloponnesian War which Sparta fights against the Athenians. Then one day you are wounded in battle. Still, you rise up to fight again. You live only for battle.

Only when you are old do you leave the Spartan army. Now you sit under an olive tree and talk about the battles you have fought. You will not talk about anything else. You cannot think of anything else.

■ ***Turn to page 109.***

When you meet the grim-faced overseer who demands to know where you have been for more than two days, you say sadly, "I lost my courage and disobeyed my orders. I did not try to rob a helot. I went back home, but my noble parents showed me the wrong of my ways."

"To deliberately disobey an order is the most serious crime," says the overseer. "A true Spartan obeys at all times. To disobey is to undermine the very foundation of Sparta."

"I committed a terrible wrong," you say.

You are severely whipped for your offense. Then, with blood still streaming from your back, you are sent into the wilderness to live by your wits for ten days. You must hunt your food and sleep in the brush. But the burning pain from the wounds of the flogging makes it impossible to sleep.

You survive at first by eating insects and drinking water from a stream. Then you grow feverish. The wounds on your back become infected. You bathe in the creek, but it does not cool your fever.

You lie down and remember long-ago days. You remember when you were very small. A baby sister was born in your house. You were very excited. But your parents did not seem happy.

"The child is weak," said your mother.

"It does not look good," said your father.

The elders came to inspect the baby. In Sparta boy babies had to be healthy so they could grow up to be soldiers. Girl babies had to be healthy so they could grow up and be the mothers of soldiers. The elders said, "The child is unfit to live."

Your parents carried your baby sister to the hillside. You wondered why they did that. They did not bring the baby back with them when they came home. You knew what happened then. The baby had been left to die. You would not see your baby sister again.

And now you are dying, too. You slip into the stream to cool yourself. Slowly the water closes over you.

■ ***Turn to page 109.***

Sparta

The main activity in Sparta was war. The whole city-state was a military camp. Every male citizen was a soldier. The boys lived in army barracks from age seven and they were allowed no other interests. They spent all their adult lives in the army. Only when they were too old to fight were they allowed to live in their own homes. Sparta was very strong. They usually won every battle they fought. But there was little culture in Sparta. Unlike the Athenians, the Spartans had no music, dance, theater, or even happy everyday activities. Many people compare Sparta to some modern dictatorships.

Matching

______	1. Spartan youth were not allowed to wear	a) helots
______	2. Spartan men spent their adult lives as	b) Athens
______	3. In Sparta serfs were called	c) shoes or sandals
______	4. The main activity in Sparta was	d) war
______	5. Music, dance, and the theater could be found in	e) soldiers

Group Activities

1. Discuss Spartan society. Was it a hard place to live? What good qualities did it have?
2. Discuss what is happening in Greece today. Is life in Greece more like Athens or Sparta today? Discuss today's Greek government, economic situation, and level of education.
3. What modern societies are like Sparta? Are there any? What did the Spartans think about people who were not strong? How does this compare with the way we look at people who are handicapped today? Is there a danger that our society could become more like Sparta?

Individual Activities

1. Imagine you are a Spartan youth who has just arrived in camp. Describe how you feel in one paragraph.
2. Find a map of ancient Greece and copy it to show Sparta and Athens.
3. Find a list of classical Greek words and write the classical Greek word for *child, city, father,* and *mother.*

The Persian Plot— 522 B.C.

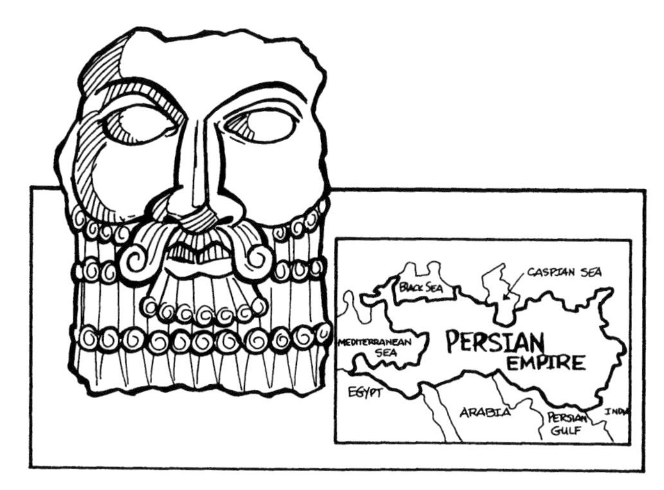

You are a young member of the Persian royal family. Soon a spouse will be chosen for you. You will raise royal children and enjoy a comfortable life.

Persia's great empire stretches from India to Greece. You believe it is the most important empire in all the world. For many years the wise Cyrus the Great led Persia. Now his son, Cambyses II, rules.

Right now Cambyses is in the Egyptian part of the empire. You live in the limestone palace at Pasargadae in southern Persia. How you enjoy roaming among the lovely terraces and columns! You also enjoy gossiping with young maidens who are your cousins. Sometimes you even gossip with the servants.

Today, however, the gossip is frightening.

"The king has slain his brother," your cousin whispers. "Smerdis was murdered before the king even left for Egypt."

You have not seen Smerdis around lately. So that is why!

"That is not all," says your cousin. "Some wonder about the safety of Prexaspes, Cambyses' own child. There are many who say that our king has lost his mind."

You are struck with horror. Could such an awful charge be true?

"A servant told me that Cambyses is in Egypt right now opening up all the Egyptian tombs. He is looking for treasures that were buried with the dead," cries your cousin.

Suddenly you notice two nobles staring at you from the garden. They look menacing. Did they overhear any of your conversation?

Your cousin darts away, but you walk boldly down the path through the garden. Are these nobles loyal to Cambyses even though he has gone mad? Or are they plotting against him?

"Gentle creature," says one of the nobles as you draw near. "Do you share our fears that our king is a threat to us all? Do not be afraid to speak the truth, young one."

- ***If you admit you share those fears,*** ***turn to page 113.***

- ***If you refuse to admit to an opinion,*** ***turn to page 114.***

Find out what your fate is!

"Yes, I share your misgivings," you say. "I have heard of cruel and savage deeds of his. But what can be done, especially by one as weak as I?"

The nobles look at one another. They seem to be trying to decide if you can be trusted. After all, you are a member of the royal family.

The oldest noble comes forward, his face flushed with emotion. "Young one, 50,000 of our finest Persian soldiers have already perished in Egypt. The mad king hungers for the treasures of the dead! He will stop at nothing. There will come a sad day when there are no Persian soldiers left to carry out his wild schemes."

The other noble nods vigorously. "Even Roxana, the lovely wife of Cambyses, is in danger," she says. "He may kill her. He would strike at this woman. Such a man is he. And he would not even stop at that. He may kill his own child, Prexaspes. I tell you, he has indeed gone mad."

You cannot believe your uncle would kill his wife and son. Why, Roxana has told you of the great love she shares with Cambyses. No! These nobles lie. You are now sure that the stories your cousin told you were false as well.

"We intend to choose a noble among us who will take command while the mad king is in Egypt," says the older noble. "When Cambyses returns, we will slay him!"

Your blood chills. They are plotting murder against your uncle!

Your shocked face betrays you.

"Look! The young one does not believe. We shall be betrayed!" cries the younger noble.

You whirl and run from the nobles. You must escape and warn the king.

You would find safety if you reached your royal chambers. Your relatives would protect you. But to get there you must run up many steps with the nobles at your heels. Perhaps you would be wiser to dart into a brushy part of the garden and hide behind an ornamental jar.

■ ***If you run toward your chambers, turn to page 117.***

■ ***If you try to hide in the garden, turn to page 118.***

"I know nothing of what goes on at the palace," you murmur. "I lead a sheltered life. It is not becoming to be involved in such things." You smile as foolishly as you can and say, "Pray tell me, is that a songbird I hear?"

"Ah, perhaps," mutters the older noble. Does he think you are a fool or a liar?

"I believe I will go to the mausoleum of Cyrus and pay my respects," you say.

"Excellent," says the younger noble. "Respect for the dead is a fine quality in the young."

You are a Zoroastrian, as is your entire family. You believe in this philosophy: The thought well thought, the word well spoken, the deed well done.

You scamper up the grassy hill. There you find the simple limestone building of Cyrus's tomb. It is thirty-six feet high and it rests on a platform with six steps. A huge carved angel with mighty wings stands guard.

You read the words on the tomb as you have often done before.

> *O man—whoever you are and wherever you come— for I know that you will come—I am Cyrus who gave the Persians their empire. Do not grudge me this patch of earth that covers my body.*

You remember Cyrus, your noble relative. You wish he were still alive. You wish Cambyses were as good a ruler as Cyrus. You are sure Cyrus is happy now in the afterlife. But you wish his subjects here in Persia could be happier than they are.

You start down the hill after a while at the tomb. As you walk, you see a dark figure hiding behind a tree. Is it just a shy pilgrim who has come to pay his respects at the tomb of Cyrus? Or is it an assassin who waits to strike you down? Perhaps the nobles did not believe your simple-minded story. Perhaps in their fear and hatred of Cambyses they would like to kill you, too.

■ ***If you continue along the path, turn to page 115.***

■ ***If you turn and run home the back way, turn to page 116.***

You continue down the path, sure that the man is just a pilgrim. It does not become someone of royal blood—even one as weak as you—to run from shadows.

But the man springs at you with a dagger! You are agile and you leap aside. The would-be assassin loses his balance and tumbles down a hill. He lands in a heap below.

Now you know what you are up against! These wicked nobles are plotting to kill your uncle and his whole family, including you! You run as fast as you can to the palace. There you find two trusted servants.

"Please help me at once," you say. "Prepare the chariot and take me to my great uncle, the king. We shall go first to Ecbatana, where I have many friends. We will gather an army of loyal nobles, then go to Egypt."

The servants ready the chariot and soon you are speeding towards Ecbatana. The palace there is encircled by seven walls of different colors—white, black, scarlet, blue and orange for the outer walls, and silver and gold for the inner walls. You gather loyal nobles and ride on toward Egypt.

But you are soon met by a messenger coming in the opposite direction. "Child!" he cries, "the king is dead!"

You gasp, "How did he die?"

"Perhaps an accident. Who knows? But listen, tender one, do not grieve. The poor king had lost his mind. He slew his brother and many others besides. We are all well rid of him."

You are very sad. But you believe the messenger. You have known and trusted him all your life.

You return to the palace at Pasargadae. Soon another relative, Darius, takes power. He turns out to be a good king. He will be called Darius the Great. He will bring new glory to Persia.

You are delighted with the spouse who is soon chosen for you. After a lovely wedding you settle down to a peaceful life. You have many fine children and you hope someday one of them may be ruler of Persia.

■ ***Turn to page 119.***

You rush home the back way. As you do, you see the glint of a dagger in the man's hand. So it was an assassin!

You find two trusted servants in the palace and they prepare a chariot for you. You ride at breakneck speed toward Egypt to warn your kinsman, Cambyses.

When you reach the encampment in Egypt, you run smiling toward your uncle. How charmed he always was by your smiling face. But now he does not seem to know you! A soldier whispers to you, "Do not approach him. He is ill."

"Nonsense," you say. You brush past the soldier and say, "Great Uncle, it is I, the loving child of your sister."

Cambyses invites you to share the midday meal, but soon he is grumbling. "My faithless wife, Roxana, plots against me," he says. "I would see her dead!"

You shudder. "Roxana is a good woman!" you say.

A strange smile comes to the king's face. "You would say so. Often I saw the two of you together, whispering against me. And you have poisoned the mind of my son, Prexaspes. He too must die if I am to be safe. All my wicked kin must die for their crimes."

Now you are truly frightened. You decide you had better leave the encampment. But it is too late for that. You and your servants are seized by the soldiers. How rough they are. They show you no respect!

You are taken to an underground room. Several soldiers and nobles are already there. It is a sort of pit. You think it must be a prison. But surely you will not be here long. The king will come to his senses.

"How long will we be here?" you ask a noble.

"Dear child, until we die," he says sadly. "We have been buried alive. Listen to the sounds of the earth being piled atop us!"

In just a few days Cambyses II dies, but it is too late for you. You are not alive when Darius the Great, Cambyses' successor, makes Persia glorious again.

■ ***Turn to page 119.***

You race up the steps as fast as you can and escape the nobles. Soon you are safe among your relatives. You turn to your oldest cousin and describe what happened.

"Ah," mutters the cousin, "it is true what they say. Cambyses is a madman. He is burying nobles alive in Egypt. I wish he were dead."

You are shocked. But there is not much time to worry. In a few days a messenger from Egypt brings news both shocking and welcome. Cambyses II is dead. It may have been an accident. Perhaps he killed himself in a fit of madness.

A distant relative named Darius claims the throne. What a welcome change. Darius calls himself king of kings, or *Shahanshah.* He builds a new imperial capital of Persia at Persepolis. It is a magnificent place, with a forest of columns and enameled bricks in bright colors.

A spouse is chosen for you and you have a chance to travel many places. Before your children are born, you go to Jerusalem and see the Hebrews building their temple. Then you go to Lydia and Memphis in Egypt. Wherever you go, your spouse greets people by saying, "King Darius—may he live forever—has commanded us to come."

Under Darius, many beautiful gardens are built. You soon walk with your beautiful children in such a garden. The garden is walled in to protect it from the strong Persian winds that carry drifting sand that would cover everything. The gardens are flower-decked and tree-shaded, with pools and canals. The Persian word for gardens is *pairidaeze,* which means paradise. And to the hot and dusty traveler, coming to such a garden does indeed seem like paradise.

You spend your life happily, watching your family grow and prosper.

■ ***Turn to page 119.***

You crouch behind a large urn in the garden. You hold your breath as the nobles search in vain for you. When they finally stop looking, you still tremble in terror. You dare not remain at the palace. All the relatives of Cambyses are in danger.

You find a servant's rags and flee from the palace land in disguise. You will hide in the surrounding countryside among the sheepherders until the king has returned.

You do washing and cooking for a sheepherder in the hills. You are very ashamed to be reduced to this, but at least nobody is trying to murder you.

One day you meet a young Persian who becomes a good friend.

"I shall soon be a steward of the king's estates in Asia," says the Persian.

You wonder if Asian lands far from here might be pleasantly peaceful. When word comes that Cambyses is dead and there is a great power struggle in the palace, you decide not to return. You hate the idea of everyone now quarreling over who the new king will be.

"Let us go to Cappadocia," says your new friend.

"Yes!" you agree. You have fallen in love.

You and your new spouse set out for Cappadocia as the new king, Darius I, takes power. You are not very interested in the news from the palace. You are very happy in your own life. You are glad to be free of being a royal child.

In Cappadocia, you and your spouse supervise the estate of the king. You decide what trees to plant and what the gardeners should do. One day you get a letter from King Darius telling you what a good job you are doing. But you are welcoming your third child, and that's more exciting even than a letter from the king.

■ ***Turn to page 119.***

Persian Roads

One of the big accomplishments of the Persians was their road system. There were roads between the main cities of the empire. Every 14 miles or so there were inns and places to stable horses. At each of these stations messengers could get fresh horses and rest themselves. Because of the excellent roads and rest stations, messengers could travel 1,500 miles in less than two weeks. That way everyone in the empire kept in contact with each other.

Matching

______	1. The son of Cyrus the Great was	a) Pasargadae
______	2. The Persian capital in southern Persia	b) Smerdis
______	3. The murdered brother of Cambyses	c) Cambyses II
______	4. The child of Cambyses	d) Prexaspes
______	5. A major accomplishment of the Persians	e) roads

Group Activities

1. On a map of ancient Persia, find Pasargadae, Persepolis, Cappadocia, and Jerusalem. What modern countries now occupy the land that was the Persian empire?
2. Discuss the conditions in present-day Persia (Iran). How much is it like or unlike the old Persian empire? Who is the ruler, what is the per capita income, and is education available?
3. In most countries today rulers are chosen by vote. A monarchy finds rulers from the royal family. How did the problems of the Persian empire show the drawbacks of this system? Discuss.

Individual Activities

1. Look at examples of Persian art.
2. Imagine you are a royal Persian messenger. Discuss in one paragraph how you make your journey.
3. Read some of the poetry of Omar Khayyám, a Persian poet.

The Great Teacher—399 B.C.

You are a young student in Athens. You have heard of a teacher named Socrates. Some say he is the best teacher in Greece. But others are not so sure.

"Socrates is a poor fellow—a stonemason and carver by trade," says your mother. "His wife does not speak highly of him, I can tell you that. She says he does not take proper care of his family."

"I have been told he asks questions that make people think," you say. "My friends tell me that he forces you to think of the deepest questions in life. He makes you examine your own life."

"Well, go and listen to him if you must," says your father. "He is supposed to gather students and just talk. If you don't like him you can walk away."

You find Socrates seated under an olive tree. He is not a handsome fellow. He is pale, with a very flat nose and bulging eyes. His lips are very thick.

"Good morning," Socrates says to the young people who are gathered, including you. You stand at the edge of the group. You want to be able to leave unnoticed if you find Socrates boring.

"What is virtue?" asks Socrates.

A young Athenian besides you says, "Virtue is to want good things."

"So you think some people want bad things?" asks Socrates with a smile. "Don't you think all people want good things?"

"Well, I don't know," mumbles the fellow.

You speak up. "I think some people *do* want bad things," you say.

Socrates turns to you. "Do such people think the bad things they want are good? Or do they know they are bad? And if they know bad things are bad, do they still want them?"

You are nervous now. Socrates is looking right at you with his bulging eyes. It is hard to match wits with such a man. You have never thought about these things before. Maybe you should just slip away. It is easier to have a teacher who tells you things rather than asks you questions.

■ *If you stay, turn to page 123.*

■ *If you leave, turn to page 124.*

Find out what your fate is!

"Yes," you say. "Yes, some people want bad things, knowing they are bad."

"But bad things make people miserable," says Socrates. "Why would anybody want to be miserable?"

"Well, I suppose because some people are so bad that bad things make them feel good," you mutter.

You remain for another hour. You listen and talk to Socrates. You have thought about truth, beauty, goodness, and other important ideas. It's the first time in your life that you have thought about such things. This has been exciting for you. You feel more alive than you did before.

You hurry home and tell your family about your day. "The fellow is very clever. He stirs the mind! I was just a dumb brute before. I did not think any more than the cat did! Now I am wondering about everything. I want to know why was I born and what I must do to have the best sort of life there is."

Your father shakes his head. "I have heard Socrates has many enemies. His questions excite you, but they make some people feel foolish. Then they become bitter enemies. It might be dangerous to be seen as a student of Socrates. People may hate you, too."

You cannot believe that. You must go again to listen to and speak with Socrates. You have listened to many wise men. In your city there are many such men who speak on politics, science, and even speechmaking. Some are really wise, but others make you laugh. Some are called Sophists, and they rent a room and teach for a fee. The Sophists have clever sayings, but deep down they don't seem to care about the old ideals of Athens. Socrates excites you much more than any of them.

Most people you know in Athens believe in many gods. There are many stories about gods like Zeus and his brothers and sisters. But Socrates says there is only one God. Now your mother says, "Socrates will get into big trouble for saying that!"

Maybe she's right. Maybe there *is* danger in being with Socrates.

■ ***If you return to Socrates, turn to page 125.***

■ ***If you avoid him, turn to page 126.***

You hurry away. It is too hard to argue with someone like Socrates.

You stop and enjoy a midday meal with friends and you talk about meeting Socrates. "He quickly makes you feel uncomfortable," you say.

Your friend's eyes glow with anger. "He is stupid! He claims to be very wise, but my father said he is ignorant."

"Oh no," you say. "Socrates does not claim to be wise. He is a humble man. I say he is just a harmless old philosopher. I must say he made me nervous, but I saw no evil in him."

"Once I met him and everything I said he turned against me," says your friend. "He enjoys making you think all your ideas are wrong. I have heard he is a dangerous man who wants to destroy Athens. I think it would be a good thing if the old wretch were killed!"

You are surprised and shocked by your friend's rage. You are now glad you did not stay to hear more of what Socrates had to say. You have a nice life and you have no wish to spoil it by getting into trouble over a teacher.

You pay a fee to some other teachers called Sophists, and they teach you how to write speeches. You plan to make a living writing speeches for people. Many politicians in Athens need people to write good speeches for them.

You have a good way with words, and you read a lot. Soon you are writing speeches for different people. People who are accused of crimes need someone to plead their case before the court. Sometimes you write such speeches and deliver them. When you are successful the accused go free.

An Athenian sculptor has been accused of dishonesty. He wants you to write a speech for him. He is accused of accepting payment for a piece of sculpture he did a bad job on. He asks you to write his argument against the charges. But a politician also needs your services. He wants a good speech asking people for their support.

■ ***If you write the sculptor's speech, turn to page 127.***

■ ***If you write the politician's speech, turn to page 128.***

You return to listen to more of Socrates' questions. You notice a sinister-looking group of people gathering. They watch Socrates with hatred. Then they come forward and one of them says, "You are under arrest, Socrates, for destroying the ideals on which Athens was built!"

Socrates is taken away before your eyes. "It is unjust," you mutter. But another young Athenian standing at your shoulder says, "Students of Socrates have caused trouble in Athens. They have stirred up revolutions. Perhaps Socrates should be stopped."

"But Socrates only made us think," you say.

"Shhh," says the other student. "Watch your tongue. You may be accused of impiety—attacking the accepted religion."

The court which tries Socrates is made up of 501 citizens. The members of the jury were chosen by lot. There is no judge or special jury. The entire group of 501 citizens will vote. The majority will decide Socrates' fate.

Socrates makes a very powerful speech in his own defense. He says he teaches as he does because it is his way of serving God and Athens. He says it is not true that he wants to destroy the ideals of Athens. He says there is just one important lesson—to know what is right and do it.

Then the jury votes on the guilt or innocence of your teacher.

Socrates is found guilty. You are stunned and very sad. The vote is 281 for guilty, 220 for innocent.

Now Socrates speaks again. He does not condemn those who voted him guilty. He says he believes in speaking his mind no matter what the penalty is.

Socrates is sentenced to death. He is given poison, and when it reaches his heart he dies. You are proud that you knew Socrates even for a little while. You will never forget him. And now you go every day to an olive grove where another great teacher speaks. You study with Plato, Socrates' most brilliant student.

■ ***Turn to page 129.***

You avoid Socrates out of fear. Then you find out he has been arrested! He is sentenced to death for trying to undermine Athens and his young students.

"Now aren't you glad you stayed away from that troublesome man?" asks your mother.

"I suppose so. I heard that Plato, a student of Socrates, is now teaching in the olive grove. But I guess it would be dangerous to listen to him as well."

"Yes," your father agrees. "Life is very unsettled in Athens. Everybody is accusing everybody else. When things are like that, it is better to avoid anybody who is different. Stick with the good old Sophists. Learn from them and you can be a teacher, too."

Sophists are professional wise men who teach practical and useful information. You learn to speak well from a Sophist teacher. Then you rent a small room and charge fees to teach students yourself.

You are very careful what you teach. You teach grammar and the art of speaking. You want to train your students for careers. Sophist teachers do not really care about things like truth, beauty, or goodness. They say it is silly to wonder about such things. So when one of your students asks you such a question, you are upset.

"What do you think love of state is?" your student asks.

"Oh, it means doing what is good for the people," you mutter.

"Even if that means going against what the leaders say?" asks the student.

You feel a rush of fear. You must not say anything that would offend anybody. You don't want to end up like Socrates! "No, no," you say. "Do not put words in my mouth. Oh—look how the sun sinks. I must be off now. I have no more time for idle chatter."

The student looks at you with a pitying smile. He knows you are afraid of saying anything important. But you cannot be brave like Socrates. You cannot risk death.

■ ***Turn to page 129.***

You meet with the accused sculptor. He is a small, nervous man. He was paid to sculpt a heroic statue of a discus thrower. "I did my best," he says. "Now they say the discus thrower has no grace. They mock me. I am an honorable man. I would never have taken money for a work I could not do."

You listen carefully and then look at the statue. The arms of the discus thrower seem to be without enough muscles. One leg is slimmer than the other. It is not a splendid sculpture. Still, it is fairly good. The detail on the face is very good.

You write the sculptor's argument for him. You must gain the sympathy of the jury.

"My fellow countrymen," you write. "None among you has more admiration for the great and noble athletes of Greece. I pondered long on this sculpture. I wished to capture the courage and determination of the ordinary youth who strives for excellence. This discus thrower was not the most perfectly formed youth. Yet his heart destined him for greatness. He was able to win his garland of olive leaves by throwing the discus far and wide. He is an inspiration to all youth to reach for excellence even from within less-than-perfect bodies. I do not ask your pity in this case. I ask only that you honor this youth as I did in my sculpture."

You are in the courtroom as the sculptor delivers your words. You nervously watch the faces of the 501 citizens.

The sculptor is found not guilty! You are sure your words helped win his freedom. He praises you warmly. Your reputation as a speechwriter spreads and you are never lacking for clients. You make a very good living.

■ ***Turn to page 129.***

You work for a politician who seeks election to a council of citizens. He is a pale little fellow with a squeaky voice. He must have golden words indeed!

You ponder all the great speeches of the past. You read the great funeral oration of Pericles over the Athenian war dead. This is the best speech you have ever read. Then you begin to write your own speech for the politician.

Your speech is short, and you think it is very good. But when the politician delivers it he does not do a good job. He sounds terrible. Worse yet, he blames you.

"You cannot write a good speech," he screams. "You are a silly fool!"

You cannot get another job writing speeches after that. The politician is very influential in Athens. You decide to become a tutor. You work for wealthy families teaching their children.

One day a boy asks you, "Did you once study with Socrates?"

"No, never," you say. "But I saw him once. He even spoke to me. But then I left."

The boy says, "Socrates was a great man. I wish I could have studied with him."

You nod. You wish now that you had stayed. But it's too late for that now. Socrates is dead. He was sentenced to death for spreading dangerous ideas.

You make up your mind to study with Plato, the brilliant student of Socrates. You spend every spare moment you can away from your tutoring to listen to Plato on the outskirts of Athens. He teaches in an olive grove.

You remain a student of Plato until you are very old. You write some books of your own which are full of wisdom.

The men who killed Socrates did not kill his ideas after all. They live on in Plato, and in many others—including you.

■ ***Turn to page 129.***

Socrates' Gifts

The most important gift Socrates made to the world was his pupil, Plato. Socrates himself wrote no books, so most of what we know of Socrates comes from the 25 books Plato wrote. Plato wanted to keep the ideas of Socrates alive. He started a school called the Academy. One of his most famous pupils was Aristotle. Aristotle went on to write 400 books on astronomy, physics, poetry, zoology, biology, politics, and government. Socrates, Plato, and Aristotle were among the wisest people who ever lived.

Matching

______	1. Plato was a pupil of	a) Plato
______	2. Aristotle was a pupil of	b) Socrates
______	3. He wrote 400 books on many subjects	c) Athens
______	4. The name of Plato's school was the	d) Academy
______	5. Socrates lived and was condemned in	e) Aristotle

Group Activities

1. Discuss these famous sayings by Socrates, Plato, and Aristotle. Do you agree or disagree with them?

   "No evil can happen to a good man either in life or after death." (Socrates)

   "Necessity is the mother of invention." (Plato)

   "Poverty is the parent of revolution and crime." (Aristotle)
2. Discuss the Athenian way of trial. Was it more or less just than a twelve-person jury where all must agree?
3. Is it ever just to arrest someone for expressing ideas? Why? Why not?

Individual Activities

1. Read a *Dialogue* of Plato to see how Socrates taught.
2. Socrates kept asking "What is goodness?" Write your answer in one or two paragraphs.
3. Imagine you had to give a good reason why Socrates should be found innocent. Write your reason in one or two paragraphs.

Riding with Alexander the Great—323 B.C.

You are a friend and advisor to Alexander the Great, king of Macedonia. You have been friends since childhood. You are now proud to be a close advisor to the young king. You are both from Macedonia.[1]

How fondly you remember your childhood adventures together. Alexander rode a wild horse named Bucephalus. Your horse was tamer, with a tangled mane. When you raced each other over the rocky hills, you won half the time. Alexander would just laugh. Life was exciting and fun in those days. Then, too soon, you both grew up.

When Alexander was only twenty his father, the king, was killed. Suddenly your childhood friend was king! His thoughts had to turn to serious matters now.

One day Alexander calls you into his palace. "Our greatest enemy is the Persian empire," he tells you. "We must defeat them. But they have a million soldiers and we have only thirty thousand!"

"How could we overcome so many?" you ask.

"Come," says Alexander. He shows you his new weapons in a field near the palace. He has a machine which can fire huge arrows over 600 feet. This machine can also hurl 50-pound stones.

"I think with such weapons we can destroy the Persians," you cry. Alexander smiles and grasps your hand. He is so glad you agree with his plans.

For eleven years Alexander fights the Persians. You battle at his side. Once Alexander is almost killed, but his friend, Clitus, saves him. Finally the Persians are defeated.

Now Alexander is master of the Persian empire.

"You have accomplished an incredible victory," you tell him.

"It is only the beginning," Alexander says. "We need yet more land to be secure. I dream of controlling all the nations and then ruling a peaceful world."

Alexander is changing from the friend you used to know and like. He dresses in Persian finery. He insists that his subjects come on their knees to kiss the hem of his garment. Then, one terrible day, Alexander kills Clitus in a rage. Perhaps it is time for you to leave his side.

■ *If you leave, turn to page 133.*

■ *If not, turn to page 134.*

Find out what your fate is!

[1] A small country north of Greece.

You slip away from Alexander's court. It saddens you to leave your old friend, but he is showing signs of cruelty you cannot stand. If he killed Clitus, who had saved his life, might he not turn on you?

You later hear that Alexander has accused you of disloyalty for leaving. But you are safely away. You hear wild tales of his strange behavior and you shudder. He is drinking heavily and having old friends put in prison and even killed.

Then, in 323 B.C., Alexander dies of a sudden fever. You feel sad as you remember the happy days of your childhood spent together. But you must make your own life now. You are back in Macedonia, trading gold and silver.

One year you travel to the Nubian gold mines[2] to see how the gold is taken from the earth. You are not prepared for the sight you see.

Slaves and criminals work in the gold mines as well as prisoners of war. Many of the prisoners are young men, old men, and even children captured in Greece. You see the children crawling through tunnels with lamps tied to their foreheads. They claw at the the earth with their bare hands, looking for veins of gold. When they find a lump of quartz they break it up, looking for gold inside it.

Some of the smaller rocks are ground to dust in spar mills, which are machines for grinding rock. Women, chained together, turn the wheels. Around and around they go with blank, weary looks on their faces. When they slow down they are beaten. They lead the lives of brutally treated beasts. All they have to look forward to is death.

You are sickened by the sight of these mines. It has upset you so much that you don't want to trade in gold anymore. You must choose another item to trade in, or else study science and find another career.

■ ***If you turn to gem trading, turn to page 135.***

■ ***If you study science, turn to page 136.***

---

[2] The ancient region of Nubia is now southern Egypt and northern Sudan.

You hope that your friend Alexander will stop his heavy drinking. He becomes violent when he drinks. He never would have killed Clitus if he had been sober.

One early afternoon, Alexander comes to you. He seems terribly excited. "I have uncovered a terrible treachery in my court," he says.

Your heart sinks. You have seen that wild look before. "Are you sure?" you ask him. You hope he will listen to reason if you speak carefully.

"A woman came to me," Alexander tells you. "She said she overheard a man saying that I was a foolish boy without any military skills. All my great victories are not to my credit. My soldiers earned all the victories, not me. This is what the man is saying."

"What a stupid lie. Why, who would believe it?" you ask. "You are the greatest general in all the world. You are the greatest general who ever lived."

"No," Alexander says, "this treacherous man has gathered a following. Others accept what he says. I have built the grandest empire that ever was, but it will all collapse around me if people turn against me."

"My friend, my king," you say, "do not fear such a thing. Everyone knows how great you are!"

Alexander sits on his magnificent throne, his face in his hands. "I am troubled, so deeply troubled," he moans. He looks up at you. What a handsome man he is. His long hair flows backward from his brow. Most men his age (he is now thirty-two) have beards, but he is beardless. He plucks his beard to make himself look like a boy, because he fears growing old and losing his powers. "Do you think I am a sham?" he asks you sadly.

"No, certainly not," you say. "You are a great general, a great statesman. You are the greatest of men."

Alexander is now drinking wine in great gulps. You grow nervous. Maybe you ought to get away now. Who knows what he will be like in a few hours?

■ ***If you go, turn to page 137.***

■ ***If not, turn to page 138.***

As you deal in gems, you enjoy traveling around the empire. You meet silk merchants from Phoenicia and wood merchants from Lebanon. Most of your gems are from India and Arabia, but you also trade amethysts from Egypt, emeralds from Ethiopia, and topazes from the Red Sea.

You return to Macedonia and marry. You enjoy a prosperous life. There is much chaos in the empire as men struggle for the power Alexander left. But in Macedonia, the wealthy, like you, live a pleasant life. The poor want land and the slaves are restless, but you have nothing to complain about.

One day your son says, "Why must there be hatred between the rich and the poor? Why can't we all be equal?"

You smile and say, "Ah, you have been reading the philosophers again!" You remember how idealistic you were when you were younger. Why, you gave up trading in gold just because you pitied the poor gold miners of Nubia. But now you are older and wiser. You have accepted the unfair ways of the world. What good does it do to worry about such things? "Listen," you tell your son. "I have traveled widely. I know the world. People get what they deserve. If some people are poor they probably do not deserve a better life. I am successful because I have worked hard."

Your son nods. But later he takes the side of the landless poor in a revolt. You cannot believe your son would do such a foolish thing. He has left his happy and secure life and risked everything for the poor! Your son is charged with treason. He must flee from Macedonia or be killed. With a heavy heart you watch your only child leave your sight. You will never see him again in this world.

"How could he do this to us?" you ask your spouse.

"Perhaps," says your spouse, "he takes after you. Once you too wept for the poor and the less fortunate . . ."

■ ***Turn to page 139.***

You decide to study science. You have always liked science, even as a child. Alexander studied under the great Aristotle as a boy, and he shared with you many ideas he had learned.

You attend the Lyceum in Athens, which was founded by Aristotle. There is a museum of natural science, a garden, and a zoo. You read Aristotle's books on zoology, biology, and astronomy. It is astronomy that you are most interested in.

In 500 B.C. a great Greek mathematician named Pythagoras taught that the earth was a globe within a big hollow ball. The stars hung from inside the ball. At its center burned a big fire, and once a day the earth passed around this fire.

But Aristotle said that the earth stood still and everything moved around the earth.

Which is true? You stare up at the sky and wonder. Does the earth move as Pythagoras said, or does it stand still while other objects move around it?

You read a theory that says the planets Venus and Mercury circle the sun.

Finally you meet Aristarchus of Samos. He walks with you and says, "The earth moves around a motionless sun . . . yes, that is how it is, I am sure."

"When I was very small Alexander the Great and I would look into the sky and wonder what it was truly like among the stars," you say.

Aristarchus smiles. "Aristotle taught Alexander, did he not? How sad that our friend, the young king, did not embrace Aristotle's recipe for a happy life. A happy life may be found by living by the golden mean—the middle way between two extremes. The middle way between rashness and cowardice is courage."

You agree. And from then on your life is the study of astronomy. You believe that the earth moves around the sun. But it will be hundreds of years before everybody else believes it too.

■ ***Turn to page 139.***

You slip away. You cannot risk spending any more time with Alexander. You are sure he will turn on you.

As you hurry from Alexander, you see soldiers leading a woman into the palace yard. She has been crying. The soldiers are very rough with her.

"What has the woman done?" you ask.

"She murdered a Macedonian officer," snaps a soldier.

"He robbed me of the gold I was saving for my children," the woman cries. "I am a poor widow."

"Alexander will judge her," says the soldier.

You pity the woman. She is to be judged by Alexander in his disturbed condition. What chance does she have for justice?

"Wait," you say. "I will go with you before Alexander and speak for you. I have known him since childhood. This may do you some good."

You enter Alexander's chamber and bow low. "Oh, King, a woman has been badly treated by a soldier who represents your noble army. She killed him to protect her property so her children would not go hungry. I know, mighty Alexander, that you will deal justly with this helpless, wronged woman."

Alexander listens to your words. Then he stares out the window. When the woman is brought in, Alexander turns to her and speaks. "Are you the wronged woman?"

The woman bows and nods. Then Alexander says, "Soldiers, release this woman. Is a soldier in the army of the great Alexander so mean-spirited that he would rob a widow? If so, he deserved to die."

You smile warmly at your old friend. Why, there is much goodness in him still. "You are aptly called great, oh mighty Alexander," you say.

But in spite of this act of generosity, you know that Alexander continues to be dangerous. With a heavy heart you leave the palace when darkness falls. You are not present when Alexander dies of a fever. All your life you will feel a sense of guilt that you never said good-bye to him.

■ ***Turn to page 139.***

You remain at Alexander's side to help him. Sometimes you are able to calm him down. You feel great affection for Alexander in spite of his present condition. He has been like a brother to you.

One day a friend of Alexander's is taken ill. His stomach is causing him great pain. Alexander's friend goes to the physician, who puts him on a strict diet. But soon the foolish man forgets about his diet. He eats an entire roasted fowl and drinks iced wine with it. He becomes violently ill and dies during the night.

Alexander is wild with grief. You have never seen him so out of control. "The physician who was treating my poor, beloved friend shall be executed," Alexander swears.

"But your friend didn't follow the physician's orders," you point out. "The man would still be alive if he had remained on the diet he was told to follow."

"The physician shall die this day," Alexander shouts.

The poor physician is arrested and executed.

"There shall be no music in all the kingdom," Alexander decides. "Everyone must grieve as I am grieving. If any of my subjects are caught making merry at such a sad time, woe to them. All must weep and wail with me."

You quake with fear at what Alexander will do next. But still you remain his faithful friend.

When Alexander is thirty-three he falls ill with a terrible fever. You know that he is dying and you stay at his bedside to comfort him. It is 323 B.C. when he dies. "Farewell, noble friend," you whisper tearfully. "How I wish you had been as happy as you were brave. How I wish you had had peace of mind!"

You try to help Alexander's widow and her small son, also called Alexander. But there is a violent power struggle in the palace. The widow is murdered. The child is murdered. All Alexander's relatives and friends are killed, including you. You die just a few months after your childhood friend.

■ ***Turn to page 139.***

The Legend of the Gordian Knot

A legend is told about Alexander when he was a young general. He was camped in Gordium (now Turkey), where the King, Gordius, had tied a very complicated knot. Gordius said that whoever could undo the knot would someday rule the world. Alexander came along and struck the knot with his sword, cutting it. He went on to rule most of the world. Now there is a saying that to "cut the Gordian knot" is to solve a big problem with one bold stroke.

Matching

______	1. Where Alexander was from	a) Bucephalus
______	2. Where Gordium is today	b) Persians
______	3. Name of Alexander's horse	c) Macedonia
______	4. Alexander's greatest enemies were these people	d) Turkey
______	5. The man who saved Alexander's life	e) Clitus

Group Activities

1. On a large map of the ancient world find the empire of Alexander, and on a modern map locate the countries it included.
2. Alexander's most noble dream was of a government that would rule the entire world, ending all wars. Could this ever happen? Why? Why not?
3. Aristotle was Alexander's teacher. Discuss these ideas of Aristotle:
   "Liberty and equality are chiefly found in democracy."
   "Misfortune unites people."

Individual Activities

1. Draw a picture of the earth as a big ball within another big ball hung with stars. This is how some early astronomers saw the universe.
2. There is a famous cameo (picture) of Alexander and his wife Roxana. Find it and look at it. It's in many history books and large encyclopedias.
3. In one paragraph answer this question: Was Alexander a great man? Give your opinion and explain.

The People of Han—200 B.C.

You are just reaching adulthood in China as a new dynasty comes in. The men in your family call themselves "the men of Han." That means they follow the ideas of Confucius, a wise teacher. You have read the writings of Confucius. He urges such virtues as respect for parents, loyalty, and fair treatment of others. You believe in all these things.

Now you discuss your future plans with your parents.

"You are not limited by anything but your ability," your father points out.

Your mother thinks you are very talented. She smiles now and says, "I have singled you out from my other children since your early youth. You have artistic talent. You have an eye for beauty. That is something a few rare people are born with. Even when you were three you made pictures of birds that were amazing."

Your father is more practical than your mother. "If I were in your place," he says, "I would take the examination for the civil service. You might one day be one of those experts who give advice to the emperor himself. Or you might turn to writing. You could write a great history of China that would inspire others."

You are the pride and joy of your parents. They are so pleased with you. You have done well thus far in your studies. You do not want to disappoint them in your choice of a life's work.

But you don't want to be unhappy, either. You have known people who chose the wrong professions and they were unhappy all their lives. A wise old man once told you, "There are no happy people performing tasks they are not suited for."

You have always enjoyed jade-carving. You find great pleasure in creating a beautiful piece of art. But you also like scholarship. Perhaps you should concentrate on studying and devote any spare time to art.

■ ***If you concentrate on scholarship, turn to page 143.***

■ ***If you begin your art career, turn to page 144.***

Find out what your fate is!

You decide to follow the practical route. You begin a serious study of Confucius. You learn the high moral principles behind good government. After you have studied long and hard, you prepare to take the civil-service examination. You pass with very high marks.

For a few years you do minor tasks well. Then, while you are still very young, you are asked to join a group offering advice to the emperor himself!

Your father is amazed. "My child! What an honor has been bestowed on you—to share your knowledge of the wisdom of Confucius with our ruler."

You make your way up to a mountaintop where the emperor waits. Your mind and heart are full of what you have learned. As Confucius has said, "If the right sort of people had charge of a country for a hundred years it would be possible to stop cruelty."

You and the other learned scholars bow before the emperor and he calls you inside the small, beautiful cottage on the mountain. A lovely tree grows inside the cottage in a roofless space. It gives a wonderful peacefulness to the cottage. By allowing a tree to grow inside the cottage, the inside and outside are in harmony with each other.

"Our armies have added new territory," the emperor says. "That means I must have the wisdom to rule many more people. How shall I gain the support of these people? What words of wisdom do you bring?"

The older scholars say many good things. You listen respectfully. Since you are the youngest, you speak last. Bowing low, you say: "The master Confucius has said, 'Govern the people by moral force.'"

The emperor nods. He seems pleased that you have quoted Confucius. You have not been bold enough to offer advice of your own. And you carefully avoided speaking at all until the elder scholars had spoken. The emperor seems pleased by that too. But now should you say more? The emperor continues to look at you.

■ ***If you say more, turn to page 145.***

■ ***If you keep silent, turn to page 146.***

You find so much joy in art that you must ignore the practical. You immediately devote yourself to the art of jade-carving. There is great demand for jade carvings among the rich, but you can't be sure your work will meet the high standards they demand. It is one thing to have your mother believe you are a great artist, but quite another to please a wealthy and demanding customer!

You go to work making a jade scene of women weaving silk yarn into cloth. You make lovely, delicate trees, a small bridge, and flowing water.

"Oh, the sense of harmony is perfect," your mother says.

You smile and thank your mother. But now you must show your carvings to two important families who are interested in your work.

You set out in a horse cart with your work to show it to the first family. You must pass through the colony where many foreign merchants live. They have come here from Persia and Arabia to buy Chinese art and furniture. Most are honest men. But a few might try to rob you, or even kill you.

You move quickly through the colony, looking at the strange clothing of the foreigners. Some stare back at you. You suppose you look as strange to them as they look to you!

"You there!" calls a man standing by a bullock (ox) cart. "Have you local art to sell?"

The man has a great black beard. He looks like a wild man. To tell the truth, he frightens you!

"I have buyers for all that I sell," you answer nervously. The truth is that you have some small jade carvings you hoped to sell to one of the wealthy families along with the larger jade scene. But you have no desire to do business with this fierce-looking foreigner!

"I must have a jade trinket for my lady," says the fellow. "I will pay a high sum for it. Don't you have something for me?"

■ ***If you show him your jade, turn to page 147.***

■ ***If you hurry off, turn to page 148.***

Since the emperor is so pleased with what you have already said, you say more. "The master Confucius has said you must approach the common folk with dignity and they will respect you."

The emperor again nods thoughtfully. He seems more pleased than ever. "Have you still more to say?" he asks you.

"Promote the worthy and train those who are not able," you say. "If your heart is set on goodness you will dislike no person." How well you remember the works of Confucius. You memorized his words of wisdom.

"Ah," says the emperor. "I think myself good, but I dislike some men. What does this mean?"

The emperor now seems upset. You must find the right words to put him at peace. One never upsets the emperor, not if one expects to remain in his good graces. You search your mind desperately for the right words. You cannot think of anything that Confucius said that fits in here. You must make up some words that *sound* like the wisdom of Confucius.

"To dislike the wicked is a sign of one's goodness," you say.

The emperor stares at you. "Did the Master say this?" he demands. The older scholars around you are mumbling and shaking their heads.

"I'm sure he must have said this," you say, fidgeting nervously. But the emperor sees through you. He now seems very angry.

"Well, perhaps the Master did not say it exactly," you say.

Now there is a loud roar of disapproval from the older scholars. You are led away in disgrace. You have attempted to deceive the emperor. You must go into seclusion and repent of your inexcusable behavior.

Your parents are ashamed and disappointed. Many of your friends will not speak to you. For many years you remain in seclusion. Then, at last, you take a job teaching in a small school. You are a good teacher and eventually your life becomes pleasant again. But you learned an important lesson. It is better to say too little than too much. You can always add more words, but it is impossible to take back words once spoken.

■ ***Turn to page 149.***

You remember the words of Confucius on the matter of speaking. The Master said, "Hear much, but maintain silence on doubtful points. Then you will seldom get into trouble."

You bow to the emperor and say nothing more. Then he speaks: "You gave me excellent words, young scholar. I follow the laws of goodness, so I always govern with moral force."

You bow again. You have given the impression of being very wise. The emperor seems impressed with you. The older scholars are impressed too. You said much less than they did. That was a sign of respect to them and it proved you know your own lesser position. The young always speak less than the aged.

The emperor invites you to take tea with the royal household. You remain respectfully quiet during the visit, allowing others to speak. When you are ready to leave, the emperor asks you to return soon.

You are very pleased with yourself as you hurry home. Your parents are waiting for you. They glow with pride when you tell them what happened.

"Ah," says your father, "I always knew you were a wise one."

"You have pleased the emperor and made this a happy household," says your mother.

Your younger sister then asks, "What wise thing did you tell the emperor?"

You tell your sister. She looks puzzled. "What does it mean to govern the people by moral force?"

"Ah," you say. "I understood. The emperor understood. You are too young to understand."

"How well spoken," says your father.

"You are truly wise," says your mother.

You smile and return to your books. You must read more. The truth is you don't exactly know all that is meant by moral force.

You are less wise than anybody—including the emperor—thinks. But you are still learning. You will spend your entire life learning. And this is as it should be.

■ ***Turn to page 149.***

"Well," you say, "I do have a few small pieces of jade you might like."

The man draws near. He is different from anyone you have ever known before. He tells you he's from Persia. He hunts wild boars for pleasure in his mountainous homeland. But he makes money as a merchant.

"I need a gift to take home to my wife. I have been gone for a long time and I must bring something lovely to her," he explains.

You show him your delicate jade carvings and his rough, wild face breaks into a happy smile. "Ah! This will be perfect," he says, selecting a jade dragon. He pays you well for it. You feel friendly toward the man and you ask him, "Is Persia much like China?"

"In some ways. We have fine gardens as you do. The mountains and lakes are the same as here." The man laughs. "And we are all human beings, eh?"

"Yes, indeed," you say, liking the man very much now. How can you not like a fellow with such a hearty laugh? "It must be interesting to travel all over as you do. I have never been more than a few miles from where I was born."

"I came here on a fine Persian ship. It was a thrilling voyage. I would be sorry to have to remain a few miles from the village where I was born," the Persian says.

This chance meeting with the Persian changes your life. You decide that travel must be a part of your life, too. You think perhaps that to travel is to learn in a very special way.

Soon you are on a caravan following the Old Silk Road along the Great Wall of China. You eventually arrive at the marvelous city of Samarkand.[1] Then you reach the beautiful Mediterranean Sea and meet the people of Greece. You sell much jade and learn so much about the world.

You are very glad you stopped that day and met the Persian. He made your life far more interesting than you ever thought it would be.

■ ***Turn to page 149.***

---

[1] Now part of the Soviet Union.

You hurry on. You hope you can get safely through this colony. When you do, you breathe a sigh of relief. You feel very uncomfortable with people so different from yourself.

When you reach the home of the wealthy family, you enter a grand room. An old man and his son wait for you.

The old man examines your jade and nods approvingly. "Your work is fine," he says.

The son agrees, and your jade is purchased for a good sum. You have no need now to visit the other family. You are eager to hurry home and tell your family of your good luck. You take a shortcut across some hills so you might get home quicker.

You are hurrying along a rocky road when you are suddenly waylaid by bandits!

"We serve the warlord who rules this region," the chief bandit announces. "You must pay tribute or die!"

You sadly part with most of your money. Luckily you have some hidden in your clothing, so the bandits do not get everything.

When you continue your journey, your happy mood is gone. You were foolish to take this shortcut. Many hilly and mountainous regions of China are controlled by warlords who do not bow their head to any authority. You should have remembered that and remained on the well-traveled roads.

You put your misfortune behind you when you return home and begin at once on other jade carvings. But the sad experience has had a bad effect on you. You were always a cautious person. Why, you even avoided contact with the foreign man in the trade colony! Now you are more cautious than ever. You seem always to be looking behind you as if someone is hiding there.

Fear is not a good companion. It stops you from experiencing many new adventures and meeting new people. As a result, your life is not as full as it might have been.

■ ***Turn to page 149.***

The Great Wall of China

The Great Wall of China was built about 214 B.C. It was made of stone and brick. It runs 1,500 miles and it is between 20 and 30 feet high. The wall crosses mountains and valleys from east to west.

The wall was built to protect China from warrior tribes invading from the north. Most of it still stands today. It has been said that the Great Wall of China is the only structure built by human hands that can be seen from the moon.

True/False

______ 1. The Han Dynasty began around 200 B.C. in China.

______ 2. Confucius was a wise teacher.

______ 3. The Great Wall of China was built to observe the motions of the moon.

______ 4. The Great Wall of China was built of stone and brick.

______ 5. The Great Wall of China was completely destroyed about 500 years ago.

Group Activities

1. On a map of the ancient world find the Old Silk Route, the major trade road from China.
2. The stories in this section say something about taking risks. Discuss when it is wise to take risks and when it is not. Does it depend on what you have to gain? How can not taking risks change your life?
3. Discuss the following quotes of Confucius:
   "To go too far is as bad as to fall short."
   "The noble man first practices what he preaches."
   "Feel kindly toward everyone, but be a close friend only with good people."

Individual Activities

1. Write a sentence about why you agree or disagree with one of the quotes of Confucius.
2. Find a sample of Chinese writing. Write one sentence in Chinese writing.
3. Find pictures of jade carvings in an encyclopedia or art book and look at them.

The Last Days of Carthage—149 B.C.

You are a young Carthaginian living with your mother. Your father served in the army of Hannibal, the great general of Carthage[1] who fought Rome. Your older brothers fought against Rome, too, and gave up their lives. But now Carthage has been defeated by the powerful Roman legions. The worst has happened: Rome has ordered all the people to leave Carthage and move ten miles inland. How could you abandon your city? Carthaginians live off sea trade. If you moved ten miles inland you would all starve to death.

"It is the plot of Cato," your mother says bitterly. Cato is a hard-hearted Roman politician. He is jealous of any country more prosperous than Rome. "Cato visited Carthage once. He saw our fruits and vegetables growing so well. He saw our green fields and our happy people. He could not bear it! He went back to Rome and stood up in the Roman Senate. He said that because we grow such nice figs, we are a threat to Rome. And then he shouted, 'Carthage must be destroyed!'"

You know that what your mother says is true. But what can a youngster like you do? Romans surround you. You are outnumbered. The few men who remain close the gates of the city and prepare to defend Carthage.

The Romans build a stone wall across your harbor. No supplies can leave or enter Carthage. They mean to starve you all!

Life becomes terrible in your city. The food supplies you stored up last for a while, but then they are gone. Hunger grows worse with each passing day. Once Carthage had half a million people. Now there are only about 50,000 left alive. You have watched your cousin die of hunger. You have had only one crust of bread to last for four days and your stomach aches with hunger.

In the final days of the misery, you pulled the bark from trees. You and your mother lived on that. Then your poor mother crawled into a corner, shuddered, and died. Now you are all alone and the Roman legions are storming through the gates of Carthage.

Should you surrender to the Romans and be enslaved? At least you would get something to eat as a slave. Or should you try to hide in the ruins and somehow escape into the wilderness?

- ***If you surrender to the Romans, turn to page 153.***

- ***If you hide, turn to page 154.***

Find out what your fate is!

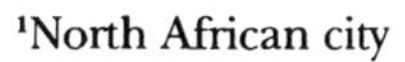

[1]North African city

You decide you are too weak from hunger to hide. You surrender to the Roman soldiers who come flowing into Carthage like a mighty river.

You are herded with other Carthaginian prisoners into a field. You must stand there and watch the Romans burn Carthage to the ground. What a terrible sight! Soon your beloved city is a charred ruin. The Romans are not satisfied yet. They plow under the ruins. And then they pour salt on the earth. They want to make sure nothing ever grows here again. And finally they put a curse on Carthage.

You are taken as a slave to Italy and put to work on a large estate where olives and grapes are grown. You are heartbroken and crushed. You miss Carthage and the good life you once enjoyed. Here you labor from sunup to sundown. You are not considered a person. You have no more rights than a horse or a goat. Your owner has the right to work you to death or sell you tomorrow. If you tried to escape no free person would help you. You would be hunted down like an animal and probably sent to the Roman arenas to be torn apart by wild animals for the amusement of the crowds.

Slowly your sadness is replaced by anger. In Carthage your family was respected. Your father raised corn and barley and you lived in a fine house. Olive and fig trees grew near your door. Your furniture was decorated with ivory. Now you are a slave.

Some of the male Carthaginian slaves who work in the fields begin to mumble about a revolt. They gather in the fields and plot. A tough fellow takes charge. He once served in the Carthaginian army and he has a lot of leadership qualities. "We will overcome the overseer and kill him. Then we will go to the house and attack those inside. We will kill them all and steal what we can. Then we will flee into the countryside and live as outlaws. Our women can go with us. It cannot be as bad as being slaves," he says.

Your role in the revolt would be to act as a lookout. But you are worried. If your group kills many Romans in the escape, you will all be hunted down like dogs. You long for revenge against the Romans who destroyed your family in Carthage. But dare you join such a violent revolt?

■ ***If you join the plot, turn to page 155.***

■ ***If not, turn to page 156.***

You hide in a stone house as the Roman soldiers enter Carthage. Only a few Carthaginians have the strength to fight, and the battle is soon over. Then the Romans set fire to Carthage!

A terrible fire burns through the wooden houses, driven by a devilish wind that seems to be part of the fire. Great black clouds of smoke roll into the sky. Your eyes burn and you choke as you flee the ruins of the stone house where you had been hiding. You race away.

Somehow you escape from the city without being captured by the Romans. You make your way inland, hiding in a silo and eating grain until you have the strength to go on. The sky is darkened for many days with the destruction of Carthage and you feel a furious hatred of the Romans that will remain with you all your life.

You find a merchant friend of your father's who lives in an Italian colony ruled by Rome. You hate anything Roman, but they control most of the world now. The local Roman provincial governor does not interfere too much in the lives of the people. You try to pick up your life as it was before. You train to be a weaver. You specialize in making caps and cushions.

When you marry, your life becomes quite comfortable. You and your spouse raise grapes, and you also make money from your weaving.

A conflict arises when the people of your region demand Roman citizenship.

"We are tired of being used. We want the rights of citizenship right now," your spouse says.

Civil war is threatening to break out over this issue. You remember the terrible suffering that war brought to Carthage. Now you have children. You just want a little peace. "Let's not make trouble," you plead.

But your spouse says, "If we get Roman citizenship, then life will be so much better for our children. Don't you see that? We cannot be cowardly when their future is at stake too."

■ ***If you join the revolt, turn to page 157.***

■ ***If you convince your spouse to give up the fight, turn to page 158.***

You decide to act as a lookout for the revolt. You watch until the overseer is alone, then you whistle. The toughest Carthaginian slaves rush at the overseer, killing him. You all swarm toward the house then. There are only two Roman women and some house servants there. They escape out the back way as you approach. You are glad there will be no bloodshed in the house.

You enter the house and steal everything that has any value. You grab coins and small pieces of jewelry, then hurry out toward the hills.

You reach a rocky outcropping in the hills and you make a cave home there. You move by night after that. The men of your group rob isolated Roman farms, stealing food and valuables. The women tend their wounds and sometimes fight alongside them.

Soon your band of outlaws is pursued by Roman soldiers as you return from a raid.

"They cannot risk letting us escape," says your leader. "If we do, then other slaves will rise up. There are more slaves here than free people. If the slaves all joined in one big revolt, we could win."

You escape the Roman soldiers for a while. But more and more of them pursue you. As you raid other farms, terror spreads in the countryside. A cry goes out: "Slave rebellion!"

All the Romans are terrified of you. Your friends and companions come out of the darkness, screaming furiously, robbing people and often killing them.

One night, as you sleep in the cave, you hear the voices of soldiers. The cave is surrounded. You are trapped!

"We must fight to the death!" says your leader. "If we are captured we will be cruelly tortured as an example to others. We will be sent to die in the Roman arena."

You take the knife that the leader gives you. Each of your slave band will fight this night. Men and women will fight and die together before the last slave goes down.

You are the last to die.

■ ***Turn to page 159.***

You decide against joining the revolt. You fear it cannot succeed. You have seen too much of the ruthlessness of the Romans.

The other slaves revolt and flee, but you remain behind. For your faithfulness to your Roman masters (which was only fear, not affection for them), you are rewarded by being made a household servant. You were trained in Carthage as a weaver and you work at this craft in the Roman house.

You make clothing for the children of the household. You have a nice place to live now and the work is pleasant, but you are still a slave and you hate it.

You think often of your old life in Carthage. The walled city contained many-storied houses. They were close together and you knew your neighbors well. Each house looked alike, but they were comfortable to live in. You remember your small bathtub and the rooms whose walls were covered with pretty mosaics. Beautiful palm trees stood in front of the houses, giving the whole neighborhood a lovely look. You remember how you used to go down to the harbor and watch the many ships coming from different lands to trade with you.

It breaks your heart to know you will never see that city again. It has been burned down by the cruel Romans and you are a slave.

"What are you daydreaming about?" asks the Roman lady of the house. "You must get the weaving done by dark!"

You want to make a bitter comment. But you dare not. You resume your weaving. You have no choice.

In Rome, a slave is forbidden to marry, so you cannot take a spouse. You must live out your life as a slave of the Romans, without family, without hope for a better future. Only death will end your sad story.

■ ***Turn to page 159.***

After much arguing, you finally agree with your spouse. Your home becomes a center for those who plot for revolution. When the civil war you dreaded comes, your sons go to fight.

The Roman soldiers ruthlessly put down the civil war and both your sons die. One is killed in battle and one is executed by the Romans.

Your hatred of the Romans increases. Life is never again peaceful for you. Life is not peaceful in the Roman provinces for anybody. Slaves roam in outlaw bands. Some rob and kill their former masters and you cannot blame them.

Your only happiness is in remembering the past. Your mind often goes back to your happy childhood in Carthage or the days when your sons were small. Now it all has ended, destroyed by the power and greed of the Roman Empire.

You have a garden at your small farm. You spend much time there. It is the only time you are even a little contented. When your spouse dies, you sit in the garden and practice Carthaginian writing.

You try to remember the stories your parents told you long ago. Most of it has escaped your memory, but you write down the things that you do remember. You want children in the future to know that there was a place called Carthage. Remembering your father's stories, you write about Hannibal. When he was only twenty-six he marched with soldiers and elephants across the snow-covered Alps. Hannibal almost captured Rome. But it was not to be.

Still, once Carthage stood in glory, and it comforts you to put it all down on paper. It's the only comfort you have left in this world.

■ ***Turn to page 159.***

You convince your spouse not to get involved. As the civil war rages, your family stays out of it. Even your two sons do not join in the fighting.

The Roman soldiers put down the uprising. You learned this bitter lesson long ago. Nobody stands long against the force of the Roman legions!

Still, your farm prospers and your sons grow older and marry. You have six grandchildren and they are all strong and healthy.

One of your sons becomes a poet. He writes in graceful Latin. He writes wedding songs and lyric poems. Listening to his beautiful poetry lifts your spirits and even makes you forget your sadness about Carthage.

One day you travel to Rome—the center of the Roman civilization. You have long hated Rome, but now you go with your son to mime shows—where people act out dramas without speaking—and dances. You also go to see Roman plays. The plays are cheerful and happy.

You cannot believe you are enjoying yourself so much. The Roman people you come in contact with seem quite nice. You always thought of harsh soldiers when you thought of Romans. But here are children laughing together and old people smiling at the sunshine.

Finally your son takes you to one particular play. He seems very anxious that you see this play.

Your son sits with you during the performance. You watch the actors perform and you smile and laugh and even shed a tear. "That was a very good play," you tell your son afterward. "I think it's the best one we attended in Rome."

Your son smiles. "I'm glad you liked it. You see, I wrote it."

You are filled with joy and pride. Your son, the poet, is now your son the playwright!

You have more than survived the cruel destruction of Carthage. You and your family have triumphed!

■ ***Turn to page 159.***

Spartacus

Spartacus was a Roman slave who lived around 70 B.C. He was a Thracian (Greek) shepherd until he was captured and enslaved by the Romans. They forced him to be a gladiator for a while, but then he led a slave revolt. He led 100,000 runaway slaves who made bitter war throughout Italy. Finally he was slain. Spartacus had led the biggest slave revolt in history and he made an important point. Soon the Roman Empire would weaken because too many of its citizens were not free.

Matching

______	1. Great Carthaginian general	a) North Africa
______	2. Roman politician who hated Carthage	b) Hannibal
______	3. Slave who led the biggest slave revolt	c) legions
______	4. Carthage was located in	d) Spartacus
______	5. Roman army units were called	e) Cato

Group Activities

1. When Cato held up the figs and said they meant that Carthage must be destroyed, what was he really saying? Was the motive for destroying Carthage military or economic?
2. Discuss the Roman Empire and how it worked. Are there such empires today? How are they different or the same?
3. Find Carthage on a map and see how cutting off the harbor could have starved the city.

Individual Activities

1. Write a paragraph about Hannibal.
2. Imagine you lived in Carthage during the siege. Describe what it was like in one or two paragraphs.
3. Look up Tunisia in an encyclopedia. What is life like in Carthage today? (It is in northern Tunisia.)

Cleopatra, Queen of the Nile—36 B.C.

You are a servant to Cleopatra, queen of Egypt. You began your service while you were still a mere child. What a pleasure it was to do the simplest service for this noble lady. Sometimes you fanned her and listened to her tales of the past. Many of the past rulers of this land barely spoke Egyptian, but Cleopatra speaks many languages. To Hebrews she speaks Hebrew; to Ethiopians, Arabians, Syrians, Medes, and many others, she speaks their language.

Once Cleopatra won the heart of Julius Caesar of Rome. You shared her sorrow when he was assassinated. You fled Rome with her.

But now is the most exciting time of all. Cleopatra has won the heart of another noble Roman. He has sent letters pleading with her to be his bride. His name is Marc Antony, and Cleopatra now goes to greet him on his return from Rome. You sail with her on a barge with a gilded stern, purple sails, and silver oars. The music of flutes and harps fills the perfumed night air. It is the most romantic of times. And as Cleopatra dreams of Marc Antony, you too have met a special friend. You know how your queen feels.

Cleopatra lies under a canopy of gold, dressed as Venus. You and many of the other servants are dressed as sea nymphs. There are small boys dressed as cherubs. The barge is a floating fairy tale! What a sight will soon meet the eyes of Marc Antony as the barge docks.

Here he comes! What a handsome, noble-looking man. You turn and whisper to another servant, "He will find our queen the most beautiful woman in the world."

The other servant nods. "More than that, she is charming. And she is smarter than any creature on earth."

When Marc Antony grasps the hands of Cleopatra he is totally enchanted. They speak for a while and then Antony invites her to supper the next day.

Cleopatra summons you and other servants to her side. "You may all come to supper. It will be all the better if you can entertain Antony and me with music."

You remember your own appointment with your friend. You had planned to slip away tomorrow evening. But how can you miss the wonderful supper with your queen?

■ ***If you go to the supper with Cleopatra, turn to page 163.***

■ ***If you meet your friend, turn to page 164.***

Find out what your fate is!

You can play the harp beautifully, and you bring it to supper with Antony and Cleopatra.

What a feast rests on the tables! You watch rich dark gravy shining from huge slabs of roasted meat. Tender vegetables and golden and crimson fruits are piled high on the platters. But Antony seems to see only Cleopatra. He is rather awkward. He tries to make witty remarks, but Cleopatra is much better at that. You are proud of how she makes the handsome Roman soldier feel right at home.

"Listen to her voice," whispers a friend. "It is like a stringed instrument."

Perhaps now would be the time to bring out your harp and begin playing. Other servants are preparing to play their flutes. You want this to be the most beautiful night of your queen's life. She has been good to you and you want her to find happiness. But before you play your harp, another servant comes close and whispers to you, "We would be doing Cleopatra a favor to make this evening a disaster."

"But why?" you ask.

"Cleopatra should not marry this Roman. There is danger in it. Many in distant Rome hate Marc Antony. There are always plots and counterplots going on. Once our queen unites with Marc Antony, she will share the dangers he faces."

You are filled with dread. Cleopatra loved Julius Caesar and then suffered from losing him. You don't want her hurt again. But she is strong and clever. Once she was a young and perhaps foolish girl. Now she is a wise and beautiful woman. If she wants Marc Antony, surely you have no right as a mere servant to interfere.

Or is Cleopatra blinded by love?

Should you try to create an incident that will show Cleopatra a bad side to this Roman soldier?

■ ***If you play your harp, turn to page 165.***

■ ***If you try to show Marc Antony in a bad light, turn to page 166.***

You are sorry to miss Cleopatra's supper, but your own feelings for your friend are strong. You walk with your friend that night under the stars. "I will be going to Numidia soon," your friends says.

"Oh!" you say sadly. You know that your friend collects wild animals to be used in the Roman arenas. You don't like the idea of wild animals in the arena. You have never even seen one of those shows. But it is none of your business. And your friend makes a good living bringing crates of animals to Rome. Once you saw young lions in the crates, peering out desperately. You saw bears, too. How angry and dangerous they looked!

"An animal hunt is going to be organized. The governor has ordered many more beasts for the arena," your friend says.

You remember the wild eyes of the lions in the crates. How they snarled at the bars that held them! "How do you capture such creatures alive?" you ask.

Your friend smiles. Hunters are always proud of what they do. They like to talk about their special skills. Your friend is no different.

"Well," says your friend, "there are beaters who go on foot. They beat the brush. The animals are scared by the brush-beaters. Then there are hunters on horseback with javelins. The animals are driven into huge nets. The nets are strung between tall trees. When the beasts are trapped, the nets are drawn tight and the animals are crated. It is dangerous but exciting work. The people of Rome must have their amusements, eh? And what is more thrilling than a show of animal against animal, or animal against man?"

You are sickened by the thought, but fascinated too. And your friend is very dear to you. You would like to run off and share such adventures! Cleopatra is an understanding queen. She would wish you luck.

■ ***If you go with your friend, turn to page 167.***

■ ***If not, turn to page 168.***

You play your harp and add to the beauty of this special night. Oh, you have never seen Cleopatra so radiant! Is there a more lovely creature in all the world? Never! How Marc Antony smiles at her. His heart is lost!

In the days that follow, you see your friend a few times. But then your friend goes off to Numidia. You share in the excitement of Cleopatra's household.

"There is trouble in Rome," Cleopatra tells you one day as you brush her hair. "I am so worried. Octavian wants power. He will stop at nothing. Marc Antony, my beloved, my poor beloved! What can he do? He does not want to leave me and go back to Rome. But he must."

"He will come back soon, my queen," you say. And your words prove true. Marc Antony rushes back to Cleopatra's side. He is sick of all the politics in Rome. He does not even seem to care about anything but Cleopatra.

But many in Rome are angry. They mutter about Marc Antony. Octavian thinks Marc Antony is a weak fool. Octavian decides this is a good time to destroy Marc Antony for good.

You are frightened to see how sad Cleopatra is. What will become of her if Marc Antony is destroyed?

At Actium there is a huge sea battle between the forces of Marc Antony and the forces of Octavian. Marc Antony is defeated!

"Poor Marc Antony," cries Cleopatra. "What shame he has suffered!"

Cleopatra and Marc Antony are together again, but their days of happiness are over. Marc Antony is sad and bitter. It seems he hates everyone.

"I want to just sit by the sea until I die," he says. He is a soldier who has been shamed by defeat.

Cleopatra tries to cheer him up. She always could cheer him up before. But not now.

The worst happens when Marc Antony and Cleopatra take their own lives. You weep until your heart almost breaks.

You had the honor of seeing one of the world's greatest rulers rule gloriously. Now you share her sorrow. Many years later you will tell your own children of this amazing woman that you served.

■ ***Turn to page 169.***

You put aside ideas of playing your harp. Instead your draw near the table where Cleopatra and Marc Antony talk and eat. You remember rumors you have heard of him. They have said his public drinking has annoyed some of the Roman senators. They say also that he has had many female friends. He is quite fickle. He likes a woman, then he grows tired of her. If you repeat some of this gossip where he can hear it, then he will probably fly into a rage. Cleopatra will see this ugly side of him. You hate doing such a thing, but you care deeply for Cleopatra. You don't want this Roman to ruin her life.

"Ah, Marc Antony drinks too much, eh? And does he sometimes become unsteady on his feet?" you ask another servant.

Marc Antony turns his head. He has heard you! It is just as you hoped it would be. Now he will grow loud and ugly. Cleopatra is a wise and sensible woman. She will be disgusted by his behavior.

But Marc Antony smiles. He even laughs. He is a good-natured person. You are unable to anger him.

After the supper, Cleopatra calls you to her side. You fear a terrible scolding. But instead she asks you why you acted as you did.

"I fear that your love for Marc Antony will end up causing you to suffer, my queen," you say. "I had hoped to make Marc Antony show an ugly side to you. I thought you might turn him away then."

Cleopatra smiles. "He has no ugly side. Though he is a great military leader, he eats and drinks with his common soldiers. He is good-hearted to a fault. Poor, foolish servant, you meant well, but you are so wrong. Marc Antony shall give me the greatest happiness I have ever known."

You want to believe your queen. But in time your worst fears come true. Marc Antony is defeated in battle and comes back to Cleopatra a broken and bitter man.

You weep to see Antony and Cleopatra take their own lives. But before Cleopatra dies she embraces you and whispers, "Wise servant—how right you were!"

■ ***Turn to page 169.***

Cleopatra wishes you good luck as you knew she would. You sail west with your friend across the Mediterranean Sea to the province of Numidia. Many Roman soldiers have been killed in these North African provinces. The fierce tribesmen often come down from the mountains and attack. Perhaps they don't like the Romans killing their animals.

You travel south into the grassland. The servants spend many hours of hard labor stringing nets across the tall thorn trees. You have the pleasure of just watching. You see great eagles soar overhead. A herd of waterbuck gallops by.

"We are looking for bigger and more savage creatures," says your friend with a grin.

In the distance you see a pride of lions. They rest in the shade of a tree.

"The lion has no enemy but us," says your friend with a cheerful laugh. "That big lion there. Do you see him? The one tossing his mane. He has lived all his life here in these grasslands. He is going to be very surprised to find himself in Rome. He won't like riding in a crate on the boat. He won't like the arena. But the crowds will like to see such a lion fight."

You stare at the lion. What a beautiful creature he is. Something about what your friend is doing sickens you.

"Do not come so close," your friend advises you. "One does not know what these desperate animals will do."

The beating of the brush begins. The lions are herded toward the nets. You fix your eyes on the large lion. How beautiful he is. His mane is like gold. You come a bit closer. You must see it all! What courage the great beast shows. He is fighting for his freedom. He charges toward you. You see his red, open mouth. There is not even time to scream. You are flung into the air. The great lion kills three people, including you. Then he escapes across the endless grassland.

■ ***Turn to page 169.***

You decide not to go to North Africa with your friend. You return to the household of Cleopatra to discover that the supper went well. Everyone whispers of the exciting news. Marc Antony is in love with Cleopatra.

The beautiful queen is radiant with happiness. You have always marveled at her wit and charm. She can speak many languages with ease. You are glad for her joy, but you are afraid. Marc Antony has many rivals in Rome. You hope he does not drag Cleopatra into his troubles.

Cleopatra's lovely, musical voice echoes through the palace as she speaks of her future plans. When Marc Antony comes to her side, you must admit they are a striking pair. He is strong and handsome. She is equally strong and beautiful.

As you listen to Cleopatra and Marc Antony talking one night, a messenger comes to you with sad news. Your dear friend has been killed in Numidia hunting wild beasts. You are crushed with sorrow.

Why didn't you go with the one you loved? Then you could be as happy as Cleopatra is tonight.

You cover your sorrow and continue to serve your queen. But her own joy is fading too. She cries with you and says, "Marc Antony must go to Rome and fight men who would destroy him."

When Marc Antony is defeated by his enemies, he returns a bitter man. He wants only to sit and sulk. And then he takes his own life.

You must perform one last sad duty for your queen. You must assist her as she poisons herself. You can hardly bear it. You so love and admire her!

You stand in the warm Egyptian night and wonder what your future holds. You know you must be brave. One day you will find a new friend to love. You will have children and you will tell them of Cleopatra.

"I served a most beautiful woman—Cleopatra, queen of the Nile," you will say with pride.

■ ***Turn to page 169.***

Strong Women of Egypt

Long before Cleopatra was queen of the Nile, a woman named Hatshepsut became a pharaoh. When her husband died in 1504 B.C. she seized the throne. She took on all the duties of the pharaoh. She even dressed like a male pharaoh and she ruled for 20 years.

Another strong and beautiful Egyptian woman was Nefertiti, wife of Akhenaton. Nefertiti means "a beautiful woman comes." Not only was Nefertiti beautiful, but her strong religious ideas were very important in Egypt. She believed in a religion that stressed truth and love.

Matching

______	1. Cleopatra loved Marc Antony and	a) pharaoh
______	2. Sometimes Cleopatra dressed like	b) Venus
______	3. Hatshepsut took on all the duties of a	c) Akhenaton
______	4. Her name means "a beautiful woman comes"	d) Nefertiti
______	5. Nefertiti believed in a religion of truth and love and her husband was	e) Julius Caesar

Group Activities

1. William Shakespeare wrote a play titled *Antony and Cleopatra.* Read part of it in class.
2. Are there women who rule countries today? Discuss why a woman might make a stronger/weaker, better/worse leader.
3. Do you think the wild animal shows of Rome were like anything in the world today? Are animal shows a good or bad idea?

Individual Activities

1. In one paragraph write about one of the following:
   Julius Caesar   a gladiator
2. Look at a picture of Nefertiti. Describe in one paragraph how she is similar to or different from a beautiful woman of today.
3. Imagine you are a servant of Cleopatra. Describe her in one or two paragraphs.

The Persecution— A.D. 210

You live in Rome with your family. You are a Christian. Most of the people in Rome still follow the old Roman religion.

"Our emperor, Septimius Severus, is a harsh man," your father says. "He has put out a command to persecute Christians. He says we are not good citizens."

You feel very sad. Long ago, when the Christian religion was very young, a Roman emperor named Nero killed many Christians. Some were thrown to the wild animals in the arena. Some were burned alive in Nero's gardens. Christians in Rome pray in secret now. Some emperors just ignored the Christians, but some are trouble. It looks as if Septimius Severus will be bad.

It is your job to take jars of olive oil down to the market every day. Your family makes olive oil from the olives owned by another Roman family. You are not rich, but you make enough for your needs.

Today, as you load the jars on a cart, you are nervous. Last week you met a new friend, a young Roman about your age. You talked about many things. But you did not mention your religion.

You are afraid you will meet your friend again today. What if the subject of religion comes up? You don't want to get yourself and your family in trouble. But on the other hand you cannot pretend you believe in the old Roman religion. Perhaps it is best if you just avoid the friend. You don't want to answer questions about what you believe in.

You look around as you near the marketplace. You hope your friend is not here today. That would make everything simpler.

"Hello!" comes a friendly voice from behind some baskets of ripe fruit. It is your friend!

Should you pretend you didn't hear the greeting and dart away behind some of the other stalls?

■ *If you hurry away, turn to page 173.*

■ *If you don't, turn to page 174.*

Find out what your fate is!

You rush around the corner behind a stall where men are unloading loaves of bread. You wait until your friend is gone before you deliver the olive oil.

"Good," says the shopkeeper as you unload the oil. "Good quality as usual."

You extract the oil from the olives by crushing the fruit with huge stone rollers. Then you put the mashed olives between cloth mats and squeeze them. Fine oil from the ripe olives flows into the jars at the end of the process. You smile at the shopkeeper and collect your money.

Suddenly the shopkeeper leans toward you and asks, "Are you people Christians?"

You turn numb. What can you say? You will not deny what you are. "Yes," you admit softly.

"Ah," says the shopkeeper. "My nephew is a Christian. He studied the law but now he has lost the right to be a lawyer. How foolish he was. I do not understand how he could have made this decision."

"My parents say that you must do what you believe is right," you say.

"I try to avoid trouble at all costs," says the shopkeeper. "If I am asked to bow down before the emperor I will do it. If I am asked to pay homage to the gods and goddesses of Rome, I will do so. I will gladly attend the rites to the goddess Diana on the Palatine hill if this will keep the peace."

You say nothing to the man. You turn and head for home. You are just about grown, and old enough to set out on your own to any distant place. You wonder if you should.

You talk this over with your parents when you arrive home. Your father says, "I think life in Britain would be safer and more peaceful. The Romans will not bother to persecute Christians there."

"I have often thought of going to Alexandria in Egypt," you say. "I have heard there is much learning there and I may study science."

Your parents are sorry to see you go so far away, but they agree it is not safe in Rome.

■ ***If you go to Alexandria, turn to page 175.***

■ ***If you go to Britain, turn to page 176.***

You go to your friend and return his greeting. "I hope the olive oil sells for a good price today," you say.

"Could anything go wrong on such a splendid day?" cries your friend. He seems in high spirits today. "How the sun shines on our great buildings. Do you realize how lucky we are to be Roman? Why, half the world yearns for Roman citizenship, and we have it!"

"Yes," you say, unloading your jars of olive oil.

"Everything that is civilized is Roman. The Mediterranean is our lake. We may travel as we wish to the Black Sea, along the rivers of Europe, down to the Nile!" your friend goes on. "And we have regiments of firemen to keep us safe from fires or dig us out if an earthquake strikes."

"It is comforting to know that these good people stand ready to help in times of emergency," you agree.

"My friend," says the young man, "is something wrong? Your heart does not seem to be in your words. What has put a frown on your face on such a fine day?"

"Well," you say carefully, "not everyone in Rome is as fortunate as others might be. The poor must struggle . . . and the Christians are in great difficulty . . ."

"The poor? Why the emperor is more than generous in giving free grain, even free medical treatment, to the poor. As for those Christians—why must they be so different from the rest of us? We all honor the emperor, but they refuse. And they will not serve in the Roman army. What sort of citizens will not defend their country? Can you imagine such a thing?" Your friend seems quite angry now.

You feel nervous. You are sorry you even mentioned the subject. You really wanted to test how he felt without admitting anything. Now you say, "Those Christians say we are all brothers and sisters, even people from different countries. They say we must not harm one another."

"You seem to know very much about these Christians," says your friend. "Is it possible you are one of them?"

■ ***If you say yes, turn to page 177.***

■ ***If you say no, turn to page 178.***

You bid farewell to your family and set out for Alexandria. You move swiftly down the well-made Roman roads until you reach the seacoast. The beautiful clear Mediterranean glitters in the sunlight as you board a ship for Alexandria. Your parents have given you a small amount of money to tide you over until you find an occupation.

Soon you arrive in the city built almost 500 years earlier by Alexander the Great. Alexandria has been a great cultural center in the Mediterranean for a long time.

You stare at Pharos, the lighthouse on the island near Alexandria. It stands 400 feet high. At the top is a great balcony. You are surprised to see fire burning there in a brass pan. A large mirror reflects the flames.

"You see," explains a fellow passenger on the ship, "the light can be seen far out to sea. It guides ships into shore during times of darkness and mists."

"Marvelous," you say.

"There are rooms in that lighthouse," your companion on the ship says. "Those who keep the light going must take horse-drawn wagons up a spiral ramp to deliver fuel."

As soon as you set foot on the soil of Alexandria, a new world opens up to you. You have always loved learning. Here in Alexandria there are museums and libraries. A great physician, Galen, has organized much medical knowledge in the school here.

You train to be a doctor in Alexandria. You spend long hours with your books and finally you know a great deal about healing. You pray with a tiny Christian group.

You are glad you came to Alexandria. You are happy here. Rome seems far away.

■ ***Turn to page 179.***

You travel north across the European empire of Rome. You move across Gaul (France) and then travel by boat across the narrow channel to Britain. You arrive in the walled city of Londinium.[1] About 15,000 people live here. Many are craftspeople and traders.

You meet with some other Christians, including some distant relatives. You are a very small group and you meet in secret. Most people here follow the Celtic religion. The Celts pray in groves and they have a group of learned men called Druids who are teachers and priests of their religion.

Your relatives are in the oyster business. "The Roman rich love delicacies," one says, "and so we draw oysters from Kent. They will buy as many as they can get. They must have great feasts there in Rome!"

"I would like to be an oyster-fisher too," you say. You really would rather have gone to Alexandria and studied, but as long as you are here you must do something.

You travel to the seacoast and scramble across the sand with the others. The tide is low and you dig up oysters and clams from the sand.

"These will end up on some gold platter in Rome," your distant cousin says with a laugh.

After a few years you change your work. You are tired of scrambling around in the cold water looking for slippery oysters. You study to be a potter. Little by little you develop your skills, and soon your pottery appears all around the Roman Empire.

You marry in Britain and by the time your children are grown there are many Christians in Britain. The Roman Empire has begun to crumble.

■ ***Turn to page 179.***

---

[1] Ancient London

"Yes," you say. "I am a Christian."

Your friend turns pale. "But aren't you afraid? The emperor has issued an edict against you!"

"I try to avoid trouble. We mind our own business and pray in secret," you say.

"Ah, you pray in the catacombs," says your friend. "I have heard of your secret places."

"Yes. They are burial places and there are rooms for prayer," you say.

You worry as you go home. Maybe you should not have said so much. What if soldiers come to take you and your family to the Colosseum to be eaten by wild animals?

Luckily, the emperor is too busy to persecute Christians very much. Soon he dies, and his sons fight for the rule of Rome. One kills the other and becomes emperor. Then he is murdered and still another man takes over.

Revolutions and murders tear the government of Rome apart. You are frightened by all the violence. From A.D. 235 to A.D. 285 there are 26 emperors who rule Rome. Only one dies a natural death. All the others are murdered. You decide to flee Rome with your family.

You gather your few possessions and leave Rome one dark night. Your ox-drawn cart rattles down the road toward an Italian province. You move as far north from Rome as you can and settle in a town that has a potters' guild. You have often thought of becoming a potter and you work as a potter's helper until you learn the skill.

You are glad to have escaped the upheavals of Rome. You live in small community of people who are all Christians and you try to help each other out. You are happy and content.

■ ***Turn to page 179.***

"Oh no," you say quickly. "I am not!"

"Good," says your friend, "because there is nothing but grief in following those beliefs in Rome."

You feel very sorry that you denied what you believe in. You were so afraid, though! You would not mind dying for your religious beliefs, as many Christians have. What really scares you is how it would feel to be thrown into the Colosseum to be torn apart by wild animals. How terrible that would be!

When Emperor Septimius Severus dies, his son takes over. Then he is murdered by his brother. Chaos breaks out in Rome. You are disgusted and frightened as even the Roman army roams around plundering the farms.

You and your family flee into the highlands of Scotland. It is a long journey, and along the way you are twice robbed by armed bands of lawless men. You almost die in a shipwreck as you are leaving Gaul (France). Somehow you arrive safely in Scotland.

Here there are no Christians. The local people are very fierce and they follow the religion of the Celts. They have a priesthood of Druids, learned men who are teachers and ministers. They worship in groves of trees. When the Roman army came to Scotland they could never really conquer these people. They blamed the Druids, who had a strong influence on the ordinary people.

You live uneasily with these people. You live in a round stone hut like the Celtic people do. You make a very poor living farming and raising a few sheep. You and your parents pray in secret in your stone hut. You miss not having the chance to be part of a larger Christian group. You miss the religious ceremonies of your religion.

When your parents die you are all alone. It is a grim life. You hold on to your Christian faith, and that comforts you. Then, when you are very old, you meet a group of Christians from Britain. You are so happy that tears stream down your face. You learn that the Roman Empire is crumbling and the community of Christians is increasing.

■ ***Turn to page 179.***

The Great Fire of Rome

In A.D. 64 Rome burned. Flames raged for ten days and most of the city was destroyed. Thousands died in the fire. They lived in old wooden tenements and they could not escape the wind-driven flames. Emperor Nero was said to have stood on a balcony playing his lyre while the city burned. From this story comes the saying, "Fiddling while Rome burns," which means not taking action in times of trouble.

Nobody knows what started the terrible fire. Some accused Nero of starting it so he could rebuild Rome the way he wanted it. Nero himself blamed the Christians. He wanted to turn the Romans against the Christians so he said they started the fire. Nero had many Christians burned to death as punishment for causing the fire.

Matching

_____ 1. Emperor who issued edict against the Christians

_____ 2. Emperor who played the lyre while Rome burned

_____ 3. This group was accused of starting the fire

_____ 4. The city that was destroyed by fire in A.D. 64

_____ 5. Who definitely started the fire in Rome

a) Nero

b) nobody knows

c) Christians

d) Septimius Severus

e) Rome

Group Activities

1. Nero blamed a small, weak group—the Christians—for starting the fire that burned Rome. This is called "scapegoating," which means casting the blame on a person or small group to take the suspicion away from yourself. Give other examples of scapegoating in the modern world.
2. When Christians died for their beliefs they were called martyrs. Anyone who gives his or her life for a cause is a martyr. Are there such people today? Who are they?
3. Discuss the dilemma of the main character in the story. Should you keep quiet about your ideas if talking about them is dangerous, unpopular, or simply upsetting to people?

Individual Activities

1. Write one paragraph about one of the following people:
   a) Caligula b) Paul of Tarsus
2. Write the following numbers in Roman numerals:
   1 5 10 50 100 500 1,000
3. Read a description of the eruption of the volcano Vesuvius in A.D. 79. Pliny the Elder wrote about it. He was a Roman historian.

The Fall of Rome— A.D. 235

You are the child of a Roman senator. You have always found life very comfortable in Rome. Your mother is always saying how lucky your family is. You have nice public libraries to go to, and fine museums. Rome even has a police force to protect you.

You are young, and you especially enjoy the nice restaurants and clubs. But lately there has been political trouble and even serious crime in Rome. You have tried to ignore it as you go about your life. But it is worrisome.

This spring you attended your older sister's wedding. You watched as the marriage contract was drawn up. Your beautiful sister clasped the hand of the bridegroom. Then sacrifices were offered at the temple. You all feasted on roasted lamb and wines from all over the provinces.

Now it's your turn. You marry a dear friend of your parents. Your new spouse is a prosperous trader. You move immediately into the provinces. You really don't mind leaving all the confusion and crime of Rome. You expect that life will be much nicer in Britain.

When you arrive in Britain you are delighted to find a nice villa. "Why, it is every bit as comfortable as my home in Rome," says your happy spouse.

"Yes indeed," you say. "It has frescoes and mosaics in the rooms. I understand this villa was built by a Roman governor. It has a nice furnace to keep us warm in the winter. I am told it is much colder here than in Rome."

"Oh," says your spouse, "the bathroom is nice, too."

"Well then, we shall be comfortable here," you say. You certainly wouldn't enjoy living in one of those stone huts occupied by the local people.

Unfortunately, there is a nasty outbreak of crime soon after you arrive. Friends warn you that bands of lawless men have attacked wagonloads of products. You are worried. You must take a wagonload of cloth and pottery down the road tomorrow.

True to your worst fears, your wagon is stopped at a lonely crossroads by a band of ragged fellows! You are tempted to try to run them down and go through. But perhaps it would be wiser to try to make a deal with them.

■ ***If you try to run them down, turn to page 183.***

■ ***If you stop and try to make a deal, turn to page 184.***

Find out what your fate is!

You strike the whip to the backs of your horses and they plunge forward, scattering the thieves. Your spouse thunders curses. The lawless hoodlums recover their balance quickly and leap at the wagon, dragging you and your spouse into the dirt. The frantic horses run into a ditch, overturning the wagon and spilling all your goods out. You hear the awful sound of cracking pottery.

"Dogs!" your spouse screams at your attackers.

You are still holding the whip and you strike at the thugs as they approach you. They scamper off into the brush.

Your leg is bruised but otherwise you are all right. Your spouse has a swollen face. Some of your finest crockery has been damaged. You are furious as you both reload the wagon and return home.

"It is unbelievable to find such crime even in the provinces," you say. "The Roman legions used to be able to keep order in Britain. But the emperor in Rome is a simpleton who acts like a Syrian prince!"

"Shall we return to Rome?" your spouse asks. "I liked it better there. We had more conveniences."

"Perhaps we ought to, but things are deteriorating there too. Besides, we could have a fine business sending local pottery to Rome," you say.

"The people here are barbarians," your spouse says.

"Well, it's true enough they lead crude lives. We Romans have tried to teach them our ways, but they resist civilization. They will not even bathe as they ought to. Yet I have heard that Rome grows worse by the day as well. It will not be like it was in the grand old days if we return there," you say.

Your spouse frowns. "Rome at its worst cannot be as bad as here."

After your run-in with the robbers, you are tempted to agree. And yet, you know that frightening changes are taking place in Rome too.

■ ***If you return to Rome, turn to page 185.***

■ ***If you remain here, turn to page 186.***

You halt your wagon and grasp your whip tightly. Your spouse calls out, "You fellows! There is no need for violence. We are not hard-hearted people. Just take these coins and let us pass in peace."

The robbers are clearly runaway serfs or slaves. They have escaped from a villa and now they live by their wits in the hills. You are an educated Roman who has read Plato and Aristotle and the poetry of Virgil. You doubt these poor souls could read a word! Surely you and your spouse can outwit them!

"You would give us coins?" one grunts.

"Yes indeed," you say, tossing them coins. Then you smile. "There now. We shall be off with no bitter feelings." You hope the nasty brutes will let this be the end of it.

One of them steps closer. "You are a merchant family taking pottery to the seacoast, eh?"

"Yes," your spouse says.

"We have many treasures in our hut. Would you trade for them?" the man asks.

What treasures could these wretches have? You and your spouse stare at one another. Is it a trick to lead you off into the hills to be robbed and killed? No other merchant would come along to rescue you in this isolated place.

The younger of the pair steps up then. "We have things made of gold to show you, Roman. Will you come with us?" He seems to have quite an honest face. You pride yourself on being a decent judge of character.

They may indeed have stumbled on some ancient treasure. The ignorant creatures may not even know the value of what they have. You would hate to miss out on a marvelous deal.

Dare you go with them?

■ ***If you go, turn to page 187.***

■ ***If not, turn to page 188.***

You return to Rome just as a funeral procession is passing through the streets. A dead man, fully dressed, is carried on a litter by eight men. The dead man is lying on a couch under a canopy. The canopy is held by four poles. An orchestra of flute, trumpet, and horn players walks in front. The family and friends follow, wailing softly.

"Who has died?" you ask. "Who is the man?"

"An honorable officer in the Roman legion. His regiment mutinied. The wicked rabble killed him," says a sad-faced man. "Did you think we would ever live to see the day when Romans behaved like that?"

You shake your head and hurry on with your spouse to your villa. It's a nice, spacious villa in Rome, surrounded by strong walls. This gives you some comfort.

The taxes seem to be rising every day. And the quality of life in Rome has gone down. The senators have little control anymore. When you think of the power your father once wielded! Why, you are glad he died before things got so bad. It would have broken his noble heart.

The army seems to be in charge. They put a new emperor on the throne every other month, it seems. And then the unlucky wretch is murdered by another group of soldiers. Now you have heard that the position of emperor is for sale to the highest bidder. Whoever can give the wicked army officers the most money may expect to be the next emperor!

The secret police watch everybody. Your neighbor is dragged off and killed one night for plotting against the new emperor. You hear the emperor is always imagining plots. He may be seen dancing on the roof of the palace at midnight when the moon is full.

Inflation—wildly rising prices—ruins your family business. You and your spouse have a meeting in your home. Friends come and you plan to back an intelligent man for emperor. Surely if you all stick together you can save Rome.

Suddenly a hundred armed soldiers burst into your villa. Your spouse is beaten to death with the broken leg of a chair. You are stabbed to death. And your sad children must now walk in a funeral procession.

■ ***Turn to page 189.***

You remain in Britain because of the rumors of unrest you hear from Rome.

You are soon glad you did not return, for there is wild chaos in Rome. Many of your friends are killed after being accused of false plots. You are glad that your dear parents are dead and did not live to see their once beautiful Rome descend into such misery.

Your life in Britain continues to be prosperous. You avoid the local people as much as possible. Your friends are a small colony of Romans who are like you.

You live a long and good life and leave behind children and grandchildren. By the time your grandchildren are grown, in A.D. 360, Roman rule has ended. German tribes have entered and overrun Britain. Romans living in the towns flee for their lives.

Your grandchildren run to the hills with their families. They must leave the nice villas with their bathrooms and furnaces behind. They must huddle in stone huts in the hills among their Celtic friends. It's lucky that your children and grandchildren made friends among the Celtic people you avoided.

Gradually everything you and other Romans before you built in Britain falls into ruin. The villas crumble into dust. The roads over which so much trade passed cannot be clearly seen anymore. They are overgrown with weeds.

Anglo-Saxon warriors hunt down the Celts and the Romans and kill or enslave them. Almost all your descendants die at the hands of the Germanic warriors, except one. One of your great-great granddaughters marries an Anglo-Saxon warrior. The girl is strong and beautiful, but she remembers nothing of the culture of Rome. If somebody told her that her great-great grandparents lived in a villa with a bathroom and a furnace and read books by the poets, she would laugh.

All that is left of your family in the year A.D. 500 is a family of red-haired Anglo-Saxons who are building a new and much different world from the one you thought would last forever.

■ ***Turn to page 189.***

You decide to trust the men and go with them to their rude hut in the hills. You are shaking and expecting to be murdered at any moment. But when you arrive at the hut, you find the spouses of the men and little children who look at you with wide eyes. They are indeed runaway serfs.

"Look," says one of the men as he pulls a small model boat from a sack. It is beautifully made with a tiny mast, oars, a steering pole, and seats. It is made of solid gold!

"How wonderful," you say. It is surely a piece of fine craftsmanship.

Then the men show you necklaces of gold. They look like little golden pipes. You are enchanted by the pieces. A mirror made of bronze has marvelous ornamental engraving. You cannot imagine where these men got these articles. You really don't care. They would bring a fortune in Rome.

"Can we trade for such things?" asks the serf.

You smile and nod. You know that these people have little understanding of the true value of objects such as this. Why, the Celts often throw their most favored possessions into lakes and bogs as sacrifices to water gods they believe are there. You dole out some coins, which seem to please them very much. You then gather the treasures in sacks and take them along with your pottery to Rome. You and your spouse will use the golden treasures to become truly wealthy.

After you return to Brtain you live there several more years. Then you see unrest growing. You now have the money to go anywhere you want.

You will spend the rest of your lives in Dacia[1], a distant province of Rome. You will swim with your spouse and children in the warm Black Sea and walk on the sandy beaches. All is well until one dark day when the Germanic tribes—which have been overrunning Rome, Britain, and all the provinces—arrive here too.

■ ***Turn to page 189.***

[1] Rumania

You cannot trust these men! You wave them off and hurry on with your pottery. You feel very proud of yourself for outwitting the thugs.

A group of slaves load your pottery aboard a ship bound for Rome. You and your spouse will also travel to Rome to visit relatives still there.

When you near Rome, your ship is attacked by pirates. They clamber aboard the ship swinging their swords. The loyal slaves try to defend you and your spouse, but your spouse is soon murdered. A cry of anguish flies from your throat. You are sure they will kill you, too, but they don't. Laughing, they grab you and bind you tightly. They have seen your nice clothing. They have decided to hold you for ransom.

You are held in miserable captivity for weeks and months. The pirates often torment you by dangling disgusting crabs into your filthy dungeon.

Finally your uncle pays your ransom and you are freed. You return to Rome, bitter at the weakness of your once proud city.

"They cannot even protect their citizens anymore," you shout.

"Hush!" says a dear friend from your childhood. "It is dangerous to criticize the government here. You can quickly be murdered for treason."

You live off the charity of friends now. A new emperor, Aurelian, comes to power. He seems to be a capable fellow. The economic conditions improve. The Roman currency is worth something once more.

"He is reviving the glory of Rome," says a new friend of yours.

"Yes," you agree. "He rules with a will of iron. It is just what we need."

Then, suddenly, Aurelian is assassinated. You and your friends support another soldier who is like Aurelian. But the other side wins. An old man becomes emperor.

"An old fool who will bring more ruin to poor Rome," you shout angrily. "The man will be controlled by wicked, greedy soldiers!"

Somebody hears you. A shadow hurries away. You are killed in your bed that very night.

■ ***Turn to page 189.***

A Child of Rome

In Rome some of the tombs were made of stone. On the outside of the tombs were carved pictures telling about the dead person's life. One of these discovered tombs contained a little boy. The heartbroken parents wanted their little boy to be remembered. They had pictures carved telling about happy moments in his short life. One picture showed him as a baby on his mother's lap. Another showed him as a toddler in his father's arms. Another picture showed him playing with a new toy. The last picture showed him learning a lesson at his father's knee.

True/False

______ 1. Rome had no police force.

______ 2. Rome had public libraries and museums.

______ 3. Romans were sometimes buried in stone tombs.

______ 4. Romans lived in comfortable villas in Britain.

______ 5. When you married in Rome there were no marriage contracts.

Group Activities

1. Educated Romans read Virgil and Horace. Read and discuss the following quotes by these poets:
   "Love conquers all."—Virgil
   "Yield not to misfortunes."—Virgil
   "As riches grow, care follows."—Horace
   "The best of me shall escape the tomb."—Horace
2. Make a poster showing the soldiers of the Roman legions. Copy pictures of them from history books or encyclopedias.
3. The Romans considered the Celts to be barbarians. Look up the word *barbarian* in the dictionary. Do you think the Celts or the Romans fit this description?

Individual Activities

1. Read some verses by Virgil or Horace.
2. In one paragraph write about one of the following:
   a) Marcus Aurelius b) Augustus
3. The language of Rome was Latin. Many states have mottoes written in Latin (maybe your own state). Find such a state and write the Latin motto and the translation. This information is in all encyclopedias.

The Empire Moves East—A.D. 324

You live in Rome under the new emperor, Constantine. He has moved the capital of the Roman Empire to the city of Constantinople. You are a young teacher who has converted to Christianity. Constantine has legalized Christianity through the Edict of Milan. For the first time in about three hundred years people will not be punished for being Christian.

Now Constantine is urging as many people as possible to move to Constantinople.

"It will be a splendid new city," you tell your mother. "It is built at the mouth of the Bosporus, a strait on the Black Sea. It will be the very center of learning in the empire."

Your mother frowns. "There will never be a city as great as Rome," she says.

"Oh, Mother," you argue, "Rome is not what it used to be."

"I do not agree," says your mother. She is very stubborn. "The splendid buildings are still being built. Someday it will all be as it was in the old days of glory. Rome will be wonderful again."

"More and more Germans walk the streets of Rome. They bring change," you say. "It will never be the same here. The real spirit of the Empire has moved to Constantinople."

Your brother sides with your mother. "It seems disloyal to abandon Rome. Here is where the grandeur of the Empire will always be."

That evening you take a long walk. You walk through the Roman forum and look at the great columns. This city has survived so much. All the terrible emperors and the chaos. The plots and the crimes. Rome even survived the awful fire in Nero's reign. And Rome survived Nero!

But you long to go to Constantinople, where a whole new world seems to be springing to life.

■ ***If you go to Constantinople, turn to page 193.***

■ ***If you remain in Rome, turn to page 194.***

Find out what your fate is!

You set out for Constantinople even though your family is disappointed. You must share in the excitement of a new start.

What a magnificent sight meets your gaze as you enter the harbor. This used to be an old trading town called Byzantium. In only six years Constantine's architects, engineers, and builders have done wonders. Roman villas with red tile roofs rise up from the hill. Everything a Roman could want is here. There are festivals and carnivals, and markets overflowing with the goods of the world. There is grain from Egypt, silks from China, spices from Asia, gold and ivory from Africa, and furs and wood from Russia.

Soon you are settled in as a teacher. You use the Greek language and you study the works of Plato and Aristotle. The Greeks, after all, gave the world something no intelligent person can ever ignore again.

When you are not busy teaching you visit the markets of Constantinople. You are amazed at the beautiful rugs from Asia and the fine leather from Morocco. Someday, if you are ever rich, you will have a rug like that in your home.

You walk with a friend to a section of town where there is nothing but perfume shops. "Why are the perfume shops all here?" you ask. Your friend has lived here longer than you.

"Oh," she says with a smile, "that is by order of Emperor Constantine. He insists that the perfume shops be clustered near his palace so the air is sweeter there!"

You laugh at that. Emperor Constantine probably has his strange ways just as all Roman emperors seem to. But at least he has no arenas where wild animals tear people apart. You have heard that he wears a wig and magnificent robes, but that surely is no crime!

After you teach for several years you decide to travel to another part of the world. What broadens a teacher more than travel?

You would love to see Egypt and the great pyramids, but you would also love to see Morocco and meet the nomads who walk the desert.

■ ***If you go to Egypt, turn to page 195.***

■ ***If you go to Morocco, turn to page 196.***

You go along with your family and stay in Rome. You begin to teach, but your students change right before your eyes. At first you have a lot of students, then fewer and fewer. All of them come from the upper classes.

Your students are not very interested in the Classics. They want to train for the civil service rather than read Plato and Aristotle, the history of Tacitus, or the poetry of Virgil. It seems that everybody wants to go to work for the government.

The middle class of Rome has vanished. They have lost their land and become serfs, or they have died out. Fewer and fewer Roman children are being born. You sometimes wonder if the drinking water of the city has become polluted.

There is little joy in teaching for you. And it's no fun living in Rome. You live in a fortified villa in the countryside. Germanic tribes frequently attack isolated villas. You hate living in a fort! Why, you are even fearful going to and from work. The roads are far from safe.

"Rome is decaying before our eyes," you tell your parents.

At last they agree. There is no longer a question of whether you will stay or move elsewhere. The only question left is where you will go now that you have a spouse and a new baby. You will need a steady income.

A friend of yours works in Spain as a teacher. You could share his villa until you are settled. You have never been to Spain, but the climate is said to be pleasant. It is sunny there, and beautiful.

Your uncle has lived for a long time in northern Italy. He tells you that there is a great need for good teachers there. You could expect help from your uncle in settling there.

Going to Spain would require more of a spirit of adventure.

■ ***If you go to Spain, turn to page 197.***

■ ***If you go to northern Italy, turn to page 198.***

You travel to Egypt and spend several weeks looking at the wonders of old Egypt. You see the Great Sphinx at the Pyramids of Giza. You marvel at the great casing stones that were set in place without any machinery. The stones are so closely fitted together that not even a knife can be inserted. Already you look forward to sharing your wonder and delight with your students.

While you are on the Egyptian desert, you see a tall, thin young man coming in the opposite direction. You wonder if he is a fellow traveler seeing the wonders of Egypt—though he is not dressed nicely as you are.

"Hello," you call to him. "Do you come from Rome?"

"No, I come from there," he says, pointing to a distant hill.

The hill looks deserted. You don't see a house of any kind. "Where is your home?" you ask.

Again he points to the hill. He smiles warmly and says, "Come with me and I'll show you."

You follow him to a cave. A small stream runs in the cave. There is a straw mat to lie on. A few fig and palm trees stand before the cave. It is a sort of oasis—a watered place in the desert.

"But what do you eat?" you ask the man.

"The figs feed me well. Some dry figs and a bit of spring water is all I need."

"But what about clothing?" you ask.

"I make my clothing from the good palm tree," he says.

"What are you doing in this lonely desert?" you ask. "Have you some work here?" You cannot imagine what it would be!

"I am praying and serving," the man says. "When the sick come and ask for my prayers, I pray for them. Sometimes they are healed."

"Do they pay you?" you ask.

"No, no, what need have I of money? I have all that I will ever need."

"You mean you will spend all your life here?" you ask in surprise. You are a Christian too, but you cannot imagine such a life.

"Oh, yes," says the man with a big smile. He is a Christian hermit. You learn that the desert has many such men. You will tell your students about the hermit when you return to your school in Constantinople.

■ ***Turn to page 199.***

You travel to Morocco and visit some of the craftspeople who work in leather. You also want to meet the nomads of the desert. You want to travel the trade routes used by the Greeks, Carthaginians, and Romans. You want to be able to tell your students that you walked the same roads once trod by traders from around the world. You have always wanted to see how people thrive in this dry, harsh land.

You strike out on your own, hoping you will see camel riders moving across the sand dunes. Soon you see one of the camels moving in a clumsy-looking gallop. You wave to the rider atop the camel.

"I am a teacher from Constantinople," you say. "I am trying to learn the ways of many people so I might become a better teacher."

The nomad leads you to an oasis a little farther south. You are fascinated to see how the man dismounts the tall camel. The large beast drops to its front knees and the man slips off.

You stare in wonder at the bright green oasis where date trees grow near a small pool of water. Then you sit in the shade of a tree and enjoy a meal of goat meat and milk. "How do you make your living here?" you ask the nomad.

"We trade camels and dates, but we need very little. Most of what we need to live is right here. We have goats and donkeys and some horses as well as camels. From these we get meat and milk and clothing. What other things do we need?"

You are impressed by how peaceful and content these people are. They have much less than you have, but they seem happier. You have learned a great lesson which you will carry back to your students in Constantinople. Having many goods does not always mean great happiness.

The nomads are happier than most of the people who live in the red-roofed villas of Constantinople.

■ ***Turn to page 199.***

Your friend in Spain helps you find a villa of your own after a few months. You start a small school and soon you have four students. You begin teaching the Greek classics, the Greek and Latin language, and writing and speaking. You are quite content until one day a neighbor comes breathlessly to your door.

"A band of Franks has invaded north of here! They plundered two villas!" he says.

"How many are in the band?" you ask.

"A hundred or more! My brother fled for his life. Some of the Romans who lived in the villas were carried off as captives."

You have seen some of the Germanic tribesmen yourself. Some serve in the Roman army. But you fear them. They are very different from the Romans. They are far less educated and rougher in their manners. They seem a little brutish to you. Still, you do not move. You like it here in sunny Spain.

In the years that follow, you and your spouse raise four children. Your eldest son marries a Frank woman. She is beautiful, with wild blue eyes, reddish hair, and a very strong body. How strong and healthy these Germanic people seem to be! Your own daughter is slender and frail and even pale-looking beside this robust woman your son married.

Still, your Roman friends look down on the Frank woman who has joined your family. But soon many other families are welcoming blue-eyed, light-haired Germanic people into their families.

Slowly, the old Roman life dies out in Spain and all over the Roman Empire. The houses with baths and tiles begin to crumble. Grass grows over the fountains the Romans proudly built here.

In A.D. 476 the Germanic king Odoacer will take the throne in Rome. Later on people will say this is the day that Rome fell. But that will not really be true. Long before this date, Germanic people replaced Roman people throughout the empire. Your own great grandchildren will all be Germans.

■ ***Turn to page 199.***

Friends help you settle in northern Italy and you begin teaching the children of surrounding families. But there are so few students you must soon take up another occupation. You move to Milan where the Roman emperor of the West now resides. You get a job in the service of the emperor carrying messages throughout the empire.

Your main work becomes carrying information about Germanic tribes who are pressing closer all the time. Some come as warrior invaders, but some just move into the region peacefully. Rome is too weak now to do anything about the problem.

You are on a fact-finding mission for the emperor when you discover a settlement of Germanic people in a small corner of Italy. They are living here peacefully, but they are not as civilized as the Romans. For one thing, they do not bathe as much as you do or change their clothing—they don't smell as nice as you and your friends do.

But you get along quite well with the German people. You join a family in a meal of dark bread and goat cheese. You notice that the people do not have good table manners. They eat with their hands and hurl the bones to the floor. Dogs fight over the scraps under the rough wooden table. This is far different from how it is in your house. You have a clean dining area in your villa.

But there is a vitality about these people that is missing in Rome. The Romans seem to have grown weak and tired. These people are ruddy-faced and strong. You don't really understand why this is so. Maybe the soft, luxurious life you Romans have led for so long has weakened you.

When you go back to the emperor, you do not tell him what you really think. You know he does not want to hear the truth. So you tell him you didn't find many German people. You tell him they will probably never become important in the Roman Empire. But in your heart you believe the future belongs to the Germanic people.

■ ***Turn to page 199.***

Constantine

Little is known about the life of Constantine. He was the son of a soldier from Yugoslavia and a woman named Helena. He was a soldier himself and the army chose him as Roman emperor. He built the great city of Constantinople on the site of Byzantium. Before Constantine's time, Christians were persecuted in the Roman Empire. Right before a battle, Constantine promised that if he won he would allow Christians religious freedom. He won the battle and then he issued the Edict of Milan. This made it legal to be a Christian.

Matching

______ 1. The law that legalized Christianity in Rome

______ 2. Where Constantine was from

______ 3. What Constantine's profession was before he became emperor

______ 4. The name of Constantine's mother

______ 5. Constantinople was built on the site of

a) soldier

b) Byzantium

c) Yugoslavia

d) Helena

e) Edict of Milan

Group Activities

1. Using a large map of the ancient world, find the Byzantine Empire. What present-day countries were part of it?
2. Make large posters showing examples of Byzantine art.
3. Discuss how Romans felt about Germanic peoples. Did they see them as inferior or equal? Why?

Individual Activities

1. Sketch or make a model of a Byzantine temple. A good example is Hagia Sophia, completed by Emperor Justinian in A.D. 537.
2. What is Constantinople today? What is it called? Who rules there?
3. Look at the icons of the Byzantine period. Write a paragraph about your impressions of them.

Bibliography

1. **In the Beginning**

Linton, Ralph. *The Tree of Culture.* New York: Vintage Books, 1958 (pp. 4–20).

The Last Two Million Years: Reader's Digest History of Man. New York: Reader's Digest, 1973 (pp. 15–21).

Starr, Chester G. *Early Man: Prehistory and the Civilization of the Near East.* New York: Oxford University Press, 1973.

2. **The First Farmers**

Linton, Ralph. *The Tree of Culture.* New York: Vintage Books, 1958 (pp. 21–28).

The Last Two Million Years: Reader's Digest History of Man. New York: Reader's Digest, 1973 (pp. 21–62).

Baldwin, Gordon C. *The World of Prehistory: The Story of Man's Beginnings.* New York: Putnam, 1963.

3. **A Person's Best Friend**

The Last Two Million Years: Reader's Digest History of Man. New York: Reader's Digest, 1973 (pp. 26–27).

4. **The Surprising Sumerians**

Kramer, Samuel Noah. *History Begins at Sumer.* New York: Doubleday, 1959.

Albright, William Foxwell. *From the Stone Age to Christianity.* New York: Doubleday, 1957 (pp. 128–162).

Gardner, Helen. *Art Through the Ages.* New York: Harcourt, 1959 (pp. 73–79).

Lansing, Elizabeth. *The Sumerians: Inventors and Builders.* New York: McGraw Hill, 1971.

5. **Babylon and Beyond**

Harden, Donald. *The Phoenicians.* New York: Frederick A. Praeger, 1962.

Frankfort, Henri, ed. *Before Philosophy.* New York: Penguin Books, 1963 (pp. 137–234).

The Last Two Million Years: Reader's Digest History of Man. New York: Reader's Digest, 1973 (pp. 58 59).

The Development of Civilization, Vol. I. Chicago: Scott Foresman and Company, 1961 (pp. 24–31).

Saggs, H.W.F. *Civilization Before Greece and Rome.* New Haven: Yale University Press, 1989.

6. **Indus Valley Decision**

Rowland, Benjamin. *The Art and Architecture of India.* New York: Penguin Books, 1953.

The Development of Civilization, Vol. I. Chicago: Scott Foresman and Company, 1961 (pp. 454–464).

Jones, Tom B. *Ancient Civilization.* Chicago: Rand McNally, 1960 (pp. 78–84).

The Last Two Million Years: Reader's Digest History of Man. New York: Reader's Digest, 1973 (pp. 158–167).

7. **Careers in Crete**

Jones, Tom B. *Ancient Civilization.* Chicago: Rand McNally, 1960 (pp. 165–178).

Linton, Ralph. *The Tree of Culture.* New York: Vintage Books, 1958 (pp. 117–124).

Strange Stories, Amazing Facts. New York: The Reader's Digest Association, 1976 (pp. 60–61).

Chadwick, John. *The Mycenaean World.* New York: Cambridge University Press, 1976.

Saggs, H.W.F. *Civilization Before Greece and Rome.* New Haven: Yale University Press, 1989.

8. **The Great Pharaoh and the Slaves**

Keller, Werner. *The Bible As History.* New York: William Morrow & Co., 1981 (pp. 119–124).

Harden, Donald. *The Phoenicians.* New York: Frederick A. Praeger, 1962.

Jones, Tom B. *Ancient Civilization.* Chicago: Rand McNally, 1960 (pp. 85–96).

9. **A Gift in the Land of Canaan**

Keller, Werner. *The Bible As History.* New York: William Morrow & Co., 1981 (pp. 220–225).

10. **An Athenian Dream**

Tarn, William W. *Hellenistic Civilization.* Cleveland: Meridian Books, 1964.

The Last Two Million Years: Reader's Digest History of Man. New York: Reader's Digest, 1973 (pp. 94–105).

Van Duyn, Jan. *The Greeks: Their Legacy.* New York: McGraw Hill, 1972.

11. **A Spartan Life**

Robinson, C.A. Jr., ed. *Selections from Greek and Roman Historians.* New York: Holt, Rinehart and Winston, 1963.

The Development of Civilization, Vol. I. Chicago: Scott Foresman and Company, 1961 (pp. 65–68).

Van Duyn, Jan. *The Greeks: Their Legacy.* New York: McGraw Hill, 1972.

12. **The Persian Plot**

Jones, Tom B. *Ancient Civilization.* Chicago: Rand McNally, 1960 (pp. 140–158).

Keller, Werner. *The Bible As History.* New York: William Morrow & Co., 1981 (p. 303).

James Mitchell, ed. *The Random House Encyclopedia.* New York: Random House, 1977 (p. 984).

The Last Two Million Years: Reader's Digest History of Man. New York: Reader's Digest, 1973 (pp. 72–76).

Hicks, Jim. *The Persians.* New York: Time–Life Books, 1975.

13. **The Great Teacher**

Warmington, Eric H., ed. *Great Dialogues of Plato.* New York: A Mentor Classic, 1962.

Robinson, C.A. Jr., ed. *Selections from Greek and Roman Historians.* New York: Holt, Rinehart and Winston, 1963.

14. **Riding with Alexander the Great**

Tarn, William W. *Hellenistic Civilization.* Cleveland: Meridian Books, 1964 (pp. 5–61).

Wells, H. G. *The Outline of History,* Vol. I. New York: Garden City Books, 1961 (pp. 276–309).

Jones, Tom B. *Ancient Civilization.* Chicago: Rand McNally, 1960 (pp. 282–288).

15. **The People of Han**

McNeill, William H. *A World History.* New York: Oxford University Press, 1967 (pp. 159–172).

The Development of Civilization, Vol. I. Chicago: Scott Foresman and Company, 1961 (pp. 489–514).

16. **The Last Days of Carthage**

Rostovtzeff, M. *Rome.* New York: Galaxy Books, 1963 (pp. 50–77).

Robinson, C.A. Jr., ed. *Selections from Greek and Roman Historians.* New York: Holt, Rinehart and Winston, 1963 (pp. 185–205).

Hassall, Mark. *The Romans.* New York: Putnam, 1971.

17. **Cleopatra, Queen of the Nile**

McDermott, William C. and Wallace E. Caldwell, eds. *Readings in the History of the Ancient World.* New York: Holt, Rinehart and Winston, 1964 (pp. 368–374).

Steindorff, George, and Keith C. Seele. *When Egypt Ruled the East.* New York: Phoenix Books, 1957 (pp. 36–46, 161–189, 272).

18. **The Persecution**

Bokentotter, Thomas. *A Concise History of the Catholic Church.* New York: Doubleday, 1977 (pp. 47–48).

Marty, Martin. *A Short History of Christianity.* Cleveland: Meridian Books, 1963.

Walker, Williston, Richard Norris et al. *The History of the Christian Church.* New York: Scribner, 1985.

Carroll, Warren H. *The Founding of Christendom.* Front Royal, VA: Christendom College Press, 1985 (pp. 395–429).

19. **The Fall of Rome**

Rostovtzeff, M. *Rome.* New York: Galaxy Books, 1963 (pp. 292–296, 314–317).

Lunt, W. E. *History of England.* New York: Harper & Brothers, 1957 (pp. 21–37).

Cairns, Trevor. *The Romans and Their Empire.* Minneapolis: Lerner, 1974.

20. **The Empire Moves East**

Cairns, Trevor. *The Romans and Their Empire.* Minneapolis: Lerner, 1974.

The Last Two Million Years: Reader's Digest History of Man. New York: Reader's Digest, 1973 (pp. 121–127).